Surprised by God

SURPRISED BY GOD

James W. Cox

Broadman Press / Nashville, Tennessee

© Copyright 1979 · Broadman Press.
All rights reserved.

4222–35

ISBN: 0–8054–2235–8

Dewey Decimal Classification: 252
Subject heading: SERMONS

Library of Congress Catalog Card Number: 78–74148
Printed in the United States of America

Preface

The grace of God comes as a surprise. Who could believe that God's acceptance of us happens even though we do not deserve it or work for it? Yet, that is exactly the case. The same amazing grace meets us in every critical experience of life. God is there with help and blessing. The messages in this book were born of the faith that God is love and that this love, which we meet most meaningfully in Jesus Christ, will never let us go.

All of the sermons were delivered in various parts of the United States and in Europe. Some of them were first preached to address specific needs in particular places, while others were preached with the continuing needs of people generally in mind. I hope they reflect the seriousness with which I regard the written Word; they also reflect, I am sure, my shifting moods and what was uppermost in my mind when they were preached.

The sermons are for people in all walks of life: nonchurchgoers as well as churchgoers. A few of them were preached in the chapel of the Southern Baptist Theological Seminary.

I should be pleased if someone looking for an answer to a perplexing question, a solution to a personal problem, strength to carry a heavy burden, or the joy and inspiration of faith, would find in these pages the needed help.

JAMES W. COX

Abbreviations and Translations

DEDICATION

to the memory of my parents

Carrie Driskill Cox

and

Isham Monroe Cox

and of my brother

Isham Monroe Cox, Jr.

Contents

Surprised by God

1

A Savior for You!

John 1:1–11

"Power to Become Children of God"

Jesus' own nation felt no need of him! John says of Jesus, "He came to his own home, and his own people received him not" (1:11, RSV). Is this not the story of his whole life and work?

A rich young man heard about Jesus and was fascinated, even excited, by what he had heard. He ran and fell at Jesus' feet, eager to learn from him. The young man listened attentively to Jesus; he carried on an intelligent conversation with him; but something Jesus said turned him off, and he shook his head sadly and went away.

The high priest in Jerusalem had heard too much of what Jesus had done and was trying to do. Jesus seemed to him a threat to the fragile peace of the Jewish nation. So the high priest advised that "it was expedient that one man should die for the people" (John 18:14). He said more than he knew, for he was only interested in getting rid of a nuisance.

After Jesus had been arrested and tried, Pontius Pilate, the Roman governor, gave the people a chance to let Jesus go free. He offered them a choice. He would free Jesus or a criminal named Barabbas. The people cried out, "Not this man, but Barabbas!" (John 18:40). "They all said, 'Let him be crucified' " (Matt. 27:23, RSV). And this is what we are told: "Then Pilate handed him over to them to be crucified" (John 19:16, TEV).

Did you ever wonder what the rich young man thought about Jesus as the years wore on? Could he ever get rid of the memory of one who offered him a chance for happiness that wealth could not buy?

And the high priest? Jesus was more on the nation's hands after his crucifixion than before. Jesus' death and resurrection simply scattered the fire that Jesus kindled while he was alive in the flesh.

And the people who clamored for his death, what of them? Many of them were "pricked to the heart" (Acts 2:37) when they realized that they had "killed the Pioneer of Life." Some of them, of course, continued in their unbelief and rebellion, still preferring Barabbas. But others had a change of heart and accepted Jesus as the Christ and Savior.

Nineteen centuries of Christian history have seen Jesus Christ, the Son of God, conquer the hearts of men and women. Nations have trembled at their foundations because of him. People have felt him touch and strangely influence their lives whether they wished it or not. Because of this, we reckon time from the date of his birth. Because of this, nations, political parties, and institutions adopt his name, unworthy as they may be to wear it. More directly, he wields great power in the lives of individuals today. Because of him, lives that had been empty, useless, and generally miserable have been made over, transformed into fulfilled, useful, and happy lives.

The centuries have not been able to lose sight of this Jesus Christ. Can we dismiss him now?

Ask yourself: "Do I really want to rid myself of Jesus Christ? Is there nothing he can do for my life—to make it freer, happier, better?" Someone might say, "I'm not sure that I need him. I've gotten along on my own so far. I'm doing pretty well with sin and righteousness, as you call them; pretty well, thank you!" But just how well do we do? Let me put to you three pertinent questions.

I

The first question: Can you handle the past? The poet William Ernest Henley thought he could. In his well-known poem, "Invictus," he said with bravado:

> It matters not how strait the gate,
>   How charged with punishments the scroll,
> I am the master of my fate;
>   I am the captain of my soul.

I wonder if it is that easy. Can I take over and control everything that I have done just because I boast that I am in control? Sometimes we say with a cavalier shrug of the shoulders, "Well, I'll charge that up to experience!" Ah, yes, but it is the experience—the total experience—that we find it hard to unload. No recording angel could be more accurate in cataloging the wrong things that we have done than our own subconscious mind. The sordid thoughts that we have fondled, the foul and harsh words that we have spoken, the bad things we have done, all of these things, even though we charge them up to experience, have gone down into the storehouse of memory, and they are there. Psychological analysis may give us new labels for old sins, but we may know better than anyone else that this is not quite enough. We learn some of the reasons why we did certain things, but we may still shuffle along with the ball and chain of the past upon us.

In the familiar words of *The Rubáiyát* by Omar Khayyám:

> The Moving Finger writes; and, having writ,
> Moves on: nor all your Piety nor Wit
>   Shall lure it back to cancel half a Line,
> Nor all your Tears wash out a Word of it.

If our sins of thought and word and deed were only against our own self or even against a fellow human being, then we might forgive ourselves or make amends and get the forgiveness of our neighbor. But what if, in the last analysis, sin is against God? What if, when we sin against our wife or husband, children or friends, employer or society at large, what if, in so doing, we sin against God? The psalmist had wronged himself and other people, yet he declared in sorrow, "Against thee, thee only, have I sinned, and done this evil in thy sight" (Ps. 51:4). Sin is against God, for he is hurt when we hurt ourselves and when we hurt other people.

Yet we have to say this: Even God, as some of us come to him, is no answer. It may be easier to believe that God is a consuming fire than that he is a forgiving Father. When I was in college, I read from *Life with Father* Clarence Day's comment on his mother's faith, and I have not forgotten it. "She loved God, . . ." he said, "as much as she dared to." We may see God only as an avenging judge, eager to exact a penalty for every violation of his law.

So I ask the question, Can you handle the past—your past, with its sins, its guilt, its failures—without Jesus Christ, the Savior?

II

Now let us ask a second question: Can you—on your own—overcome the sin in your heart? I am not talking about sins, but sin! I am talking about the quality of life that results in sins. Sin, that faithless quality of life, can dominate the way we think, the things we say, and how we behave. Anyone can overcome certain harmful or uncouth habits in life. Some, realizing that smoking is a threat to their health, have stopped smoking. Some, realizing that their swearing is coarse, have cleaned up their speech. Some, realizing that their lust is harmful to themselves and to others, have cleaned up their lives. And still others, afraid of exposure and prison, have quit stealing. In a few cases certain individuals have reformed because of the wishes of someone they loved and cared for. It is clear that some habits can be broken in one's own strength. But sin itself—can we conquer that in our own strength? We cannot do that alone!

Nevertheless, we try. With spurts of determination to do better and with a flamethrower of indignation at the failings of others we kid ourselves into believing that we are headed for sainthood. Dr. Carl Jung, the renowned Swiss psychologist, noted with keen perception, "When we dare not acknowledge some great sin, we deplore some small sin with greater emphasis." This applies to the small sins of others as well as to our own. How easy it is to add up the faults of our neighbors and consider our moral arithmetic some kind of redeeming virtue in ourselves! We can do that and all the while within our own hearts may be the unresolved problem of sin, such as pride or selfishness, which in the end may be far worse than the sins of the flesh that are so easy to see in others and condemn.

Simon Peter does not impress me as being one who would ordinarily think he was better than others, yet he boasted that he would stick with Jesus even if everyone else denied him. But he was too confident of his own moral strength. In time of testing he failed. Paul the apostle confessed that his own struggle with sin was useless. Of course, as a Pharisee his life was without moral blemish, but something was going on within him that he could not control. The more he struggled with the sin in his heart, the more he got into it. He said, "I find that this law is at work: when I want to do what is good, what is evil is the only choice I have" (Rom. 7:21, TEV).

New Year's Day is noted for the fine resolutions that we make; the days that follow are notorious for the resolutions that we break. It ought to be clear to every one of us, by personal experience as well as by observation, that in our own strength we cannot transform a heart of stone into a heart of flesh, that in our own strength we cannot shatter that shell of selfishness that in many ways separates us from even those closest to us and from God himself. As you consider yourself, do you not need him who said to people enslaved by sin, "If the Son sets you free, then you will be really free" (John 8:36, TEV)?

III

This brings us to the third question: Can you be fully satisfied with an earthbound view of life? This is a question to be decided early, for you it will sometime be too late to return a misused life for a refund.

It is true that many people have got beyond the idea of just living for the day. They have hope; they live for tomorrow or for the next generation; they seek immortality in their children and their children's children or in some of the noble institutions or worthy causes they have served. These sentiments are fine, but they do not go far enough. They never quite get out of this world. The people who hold these views—and you may be among them—hardly see our human problems as really evil, but rather as a cultural lag that must be taken up as the generations grow in knowledge and human understanding.

And then there are those who seem to be satisfied to eat, drink, and be merry in that cultural lag and call it heaven. A boy I once knew said to me, "All I'm interested in is in having a good time." He had his good time—as long as it lasted—and then he killed himself.

Is this world—this world that you can see and foresee—is it enough? Do you not hope for more beyond it than the triumph of your influence or the proud remembrance of your name? Do you not long for more from life than what can be seized by your appetites and passions? Surely you want to get behind all that you can see and feel and know of this earth to the One who made *it* and made *us* for his purposes as well as for our enjoyment.

The Fourth Gospel tells us of a fine, upstanding man of the

first century whose name was Nicodemus. The community regarded him highly; he was a member of the powerful and prestigious Jewish court called the Sanhedrin. In a discussion with Jesus, this man showed considerable religious insight. He appeared to like Jesus and what he was doing. But Jesus confronted him with a startling truth: this world and its ways of thinking, even if the thinking is done by intelligent, respectable, religious people, is not good enough, does not get the whole picture. Jesus said to him, "I am telling you the truth: no one can see the kingdom of God unless he is born again . . . . Do not be surprised because I tell you that you must all be born again" (John 3:3,7, TEV). What Jesus was saying to a splendid, pious Jew he is saying to you and to me: "You will find out what life was meant to be only if your life has a new beginning—this time from above, from God, from beyond this earth!"

Jesus Christ came into the world to give us a new birth, to put us in touch with God in such a way that life is made new on a different basis. That is why the Fourth Gospel says of those who become children of God through faith in Jesus, "They did not become God's children by natural means, that is, by being born as children of a human father; God himself was their Father" (John 1:13, TEV). If life begins anew for you on the deepest and most lasting level, do you not need Jesus Christ, the Savior, to impart that life to you?

We know for a fact that many persons do not recognize their need of Jesus Christ as Savior. The majority of his own people, during the time he walked this earth, rejected him. Yet some did receive him, and life became new and different for them. What happened then can happen to you now!

Jesus Christ comes to us today. Not once did he even hint that the passing centuries would make him harder to know as Savior than when he lived in the flesh. In fact, he told his disciples that those who believed in him would do even greater things than he himself did, because, as he said, "I am going to the Father" (John 14:12, TEV). He said to Thomas, who asked for proof positive that the risen Christ was the Jesus he had known, "Do you believe because you see me? How happy are those who believe without seeing me!" (John 20:29, TEV).

Are you asking, "How can I receive him today? How can he become a part of my life, so that I am different, with different attitudes, different aims, and different hopes?"

It is really very simple. Jesus Christ lives today. Never was his power to save greater than today. Never was his call for disciples—people to follow and serve him—more urgent than today. So he comes to us through the call of the church and those who represent it, saying, "Follow me." Then, follow him! If you follow him, it implies that you trust him to do all that he promised to do for his followers: to forgive your sins, to give you better things to live for, to help you do what is right, and to give you everlasting life. And let me say this: the only way you will ever take the last step of the journey is to take the first step.

When Jesus came in the flesh to his own home, his own people, as a whole, did not receive him. Neither do all receive him today when the good news is preached. "But to all who received him [and it is as true today as it was 2,000 years ago], who believed in his name, he gave power to become children of God" (John 1:12, RSV).

There is a Savior for you! Receive him today, and enter into all the riches of the blessings of God!

2

The Conversion of an Unpromising Prospect

Luke 19:1-10

"Today Salvation Has Come"

Zacchaeus was not the kind of man most people would go out of their way to save. He had made a terrible mistake. It was unpardonable, if you look at it the way some of his fellow Jews saw it. He was a publican, a tax gatherer. This meant that he was a quisling, a traitor, a renegade. He was perhaps the most unpopular man in Jericho. To get and hold his job he had to collaborate with imperial Rome. He took up the cause of the enemy against his own people. Or so it seemed.

We all know how it works. Zacchaeus received the brunt of people's natural dislike of a cheat, an informer, a spy. Zacchaeus was an odious man not only because he cooperated with the enemy, but, more than that, because he got rich doing it.

We do not have an exact equivalent of Zacchaeus in our society. But don't we treat many people as the Jews treated Zacchaeus? Jesus said that he came to save sinners, but don't we spend most of our time seeking out the respectable? Jesus said that it was his mission to draw all men unto himself, but don't we make some people feel unwelcome in our churches? Jesus said that he came not to bring peace, but a sword, but don't we placate the man of the world and condemn the so-called "fanatic"? So, Zacchaeus, with various aliases, is still among us.

Look again at the Zacchaeus of Jesus' time. He was a despised man, yes! But he had his compensations. Even some of his desdainful contemporaries could have said, "I could stand a lot of cold-shouldering if I had his kind of money." Many of them

17

could have been easily tempted to sacrifice affection for power.

Zacchaeus was not universally despised. He had his little group to whom he looked for approval, perhaps even affection. There was the Roman government, his benefactor. And there were those scattered officials working under him, with him, and over him. From them he got little crumbs of approval that kept him from completely starving for human fellowship.

What a fantastic spot was Jericho, the home of Zacchaeus! Zacchaeus awoke every morning to smell the fragrance of the balsam trees that grew in profusion and made Jericho famous throughout the East. A story is told that this remarkable fragrance was carried by the winds across the wilderness of Judea and all the way to the Mediterranean Sea. For Zacchaeus the smell of the balsam trees was the smell of money. He loved it!

No place in the world enjoyed a better climate. It was only thirty miles east of high, windswept, often cold Jerusalem, right at the edge of the godforsaken wilderness of Judea. You could look to the south and see the dreadful but beautiful Dead Sea, and to the east, the Jordan river. Jericho was a tropical paradise. Here Herod the Great and his son Archelaus had built their winter palaces. Here the wealthy built fabulous villas comparable to the expensive homes at Pompeii. Here a large number of the priests at Jerusalem chose to live. It was an ideal place for the assistant secretary of the treasury.

But Zacchaeus had a great emptiness in his life. He could hardly enjoy his money living every day under the frowns and disapproving eyes of his fellow citizens. What could a million dollars or ten cents mean to him if he had to lie awake at night worrying about how he got it? Lush, formal gardens, sparkling fountains, and marbled walls could scarcely beguile his dreams of children crying from hunger.

Every sacred feast, every family gathering reminded Zacchaeus of his great spiritual distance from his childhood neighbors, his old friends, and his own relatives. Yet he may have made a great pretense of indifference. People often do. What they cannot enjoy they scorn. What they cannot have in themselves, they laugh at in others. What their money cannot buy, they say they do not want anyway. But rare moments of insight dawn even in the most callous. The sound of carefree laughter, the haunting refrain of a song heard in childhood, the sight of an unexpected tragedy—any one of these was enough to shatter the walls of Zacchaeus' pride and send a chill of despair to his heart.

Could it be that the coming of Jesus to Jericho stirred some old, half-forgotten longings in Zacchaeus? Had Zacchaeus heard of other tax gatherers who had begun to follow Jesus? Surely word of these goings-on had been carried quickly to Jericho, and Zacchaeus was among the first to hear the news. Here was a Jew who had a kind word for a tax gatherer. Here was a Jew who did not take up the derisive chant of his fellow citizens.

Whatever his motivation, Zacchaeus was determined to see Jesus. But it was not easy. Zacchaeus was short of stature. He might own the tax franchise in Jericho, but he didn't own the streets! No one would let him make an opening in the throng and get through to Jesus. This little incident in itself indicates how unpopular Zacchaeus was. Still, he did not give up.

He ran on ahead of the crowd and scrambled up a sycamore tree where he could get a clear view when Jesus passed by. A thousand times he had compensated for his lack of height by asserting his legal power over the money and property of others. Now he did it again. He had not gotten his wealth by timidity. He was aggressive. He was resourceful. If one thing did not work, he would try another, even if it meant climbing into a sycamore tree! You wouldn't have caught a Pharisee doing this, but Zacchaeus couldn't have cared less.

There Zacchaeus was, sitting on a branch of the tree. Jesus moved slowly along amid the chatter and tumult that surrounded him. Can you visualize it? One by one the faces intent on Jesus turned away until all eyes were fastened on the funny little man in the tree. Perhaps someone pointed toward Zacchaeus and snickered scornfully. It was a ludicrous sight. But Jesus did not join in their derision. He stopped. He made a gesture for silence. What was he going to say to this man? Was he going to put him in his place? Jesus spoke, and what he said was astounding. "Zacchaeus, make haste and come down; for I must stay at your house today" (Luke 19:5, RSV). Jesus completely ignored the prejudices of the crowd. By requesting his hospitality, he honored Zacchaeus. No doubt Zacchaeus was just as astonished as the crowd. Yet, he was overjoyed.

But the astonishment of the crowd quickly turned into resentment. "There are a hundred places in Jericho Jesus could have stayed without having to stay with him." "There's the Inn of the Good Samaritan only a little way off." "I'd rather sleep outside than share the house of a tax gatherer." You can imagine the kind of things they said. But they *were* traveling with Jesus, these disciples and other companions! And it *was* a large crowd! And Zacchaeus *would* set a good table! And it *was* about time somebody got some good out of all those hateful taxes they paid! And Jesus just *might* tell him what's what! So they gritted their teeth, and they, too, accepted Zacchaeus' hospitality.

Picture these people as they climbed step-by-step up to the house of Zacchaeus. Zacchaeus led the way and Jesus walked with him. The disciples and the others followed behind, talking in hushed but sometimes scornful tones as they viewed the costly appointments.

Then came mealtime. The tired, hungry travelers bathed their hands and faces and feet with the cold water brought in by aquaduct from the valley made famous by the twenty-third Psalm. Now they were refreshed. They took their places on couches and the feast began. Jesus was next to Zacchaeus.

The two had much to talk about. Zacchaeus was overwhelmed by the honor that had come to him. Therefore, I can imagine, he was all the more embarrassed by his occupation. Think of the explanations, the defenses, the rationalizations before Jesus had said a word to him about the way he made his living. No doubt Zacchaeus argued. The more he defended himself the weaker his case became. Did he finally give up, as so many before and since have done, and say, "Lord, what shall I do?"

As guest of honor at a long, lavish meal, Jesus had time and opportunity to say what he wished to his host. Perhaps the others were too busy eating the delightfully seasoned food—mouthwatering enough for a king—and talking among themselves to pay too much attention to what Jesus and Zacchaeus said quietly to each other.

I imagine that Jesus left no sensitive spot in the man's soul untouched. Did Jesus tell Zacchaeus of his own temptations? There, within sight, was the place in the wilderness where he was tempted of the devil. When Satan suggested that Jesus bow down and worship him and promised that if he did so all the world and its glories would be his, was Jesus then looking down on the fertile valley below with its dates and balsams, with Jericho and the palaces and the villas? This would have been a good place to start—the wealthiest spot in Palestine.

Now what did Jesus ask Zacchaeus? "Friend, has your wealth brought you happiness?" "Are there people whose lives could be better if you had helped them?" "Have you considered what God may think of you?" Whatever it was, the words of Jesus found their mark. Whatever searching and probing of conscience he did, Jesus talked at the same time of something so great, so exciting, and so rewarding that anything he had to say was welcome. For all of their sharp, astringent pain, Jesus' words were good news.

Of course Jesus might have played down the demands. He

might have tried to flatter Zacchaeus and get him to give enough to the poor to put his conscience to sleep, and then let it go at that. But if Jesus had done this, Zacchaeus would have been a lost soul still. He would have been no better off. The demand was unconditional surrender, and the reward was as great as the demand.

Here shines forth the glory of Jesus' ministry. Jesus dealt with men as individuals. Certainly the multitudes thronged about him. He did not drive the crowds away. But he sought out individuals within the crowd. He had love for these persons; he had time for them; he had a message tailored to their uniqueness. Some of the yearning faces that looked up at him were the lean faces of the poor; some the twisted faces of the suffering. Some of the eyes that sought him out were the frightened eyes of the persecuted and exploited; some the cold, calculating eyes of the proud and hardhearted. But Jesus read again and again the story told by the lines in those faces and by the looks in those eyes, and he went after the individuals they represented and helped them one by one.

A miracle happened! Zacchaeus was a changed man. A complete reversal of values shook his character to its foundations. The old motivation in life died. A new resolve was born. Life had a new center. The poor, the exploited were now his concern. His heart was strangely warmed by the mercy of God and by the "still, sad music of humanity."

It was time for a solemn avowal. Zacchaeus stood up. "Behold, Lord, the half of my goods I give to the poor," he said. A whisper went among the guests. Their faces registered both pleasure and awe. "Do our ears deceive us?" you can imagine them saying. Then, not defiantly, but shaken by this transforming experience, Zacchaeus went on: "And if I have defrauded any one of anything, I restore it fourfold."

This was even more astonishing. The Jewish law required a

man to pay back only twice what he had taken dishonestly. To pay back four dollars for every one was unbelievable!

Yet this kind of response should not be too surprising. And why? Because conversion is a miracle of God. The God who created the universe out of nothing, who brought Israel out of slavery in Egypt, who returned the exiles from Babylon, who raised Jesus Christ from the dead, this God takes a moral and spiritual nobody and gives him a new name and a new disposition. It is because we still believe in God that we go to the Zacchaeuses of the twentieth century, the social pariahs, the outcasts, and hold before them the prospect of a new life, a life full of miracle and meaning. The day of moral and spiritual miracles is not past.

Zacchaeus, the unlikely convert, was genuinely changed. Jesus saw that his experience ran deep. It was no passing fancy. It was no seed springing up quickly in shallow soil only to wither as quickly as it had sprung up. New life had begun. Jesus responded by saying, "Today salvation has come to this house." What had happened to Zacchaeus was what Paul described when he wrote: "If any man be in Christ, he is a new creature: old things are passed away, behold all things are become new" (2 Cor. 5:17).

In this incident was Jesus' philosophy of evangelism. Here Jesus showed us by what *he* did, what *we* ought to do. If we do not seek out the rejected, the morally homeless of this world, and if we do not see them as individual souls made for God, then we may discover that even in our "churchiness" we are working for ourselves, not for Jesus Christ; that custom and convention mean more to us than does the kingdom of God. Jesus declared that the "Son of man came to seek and to save the lost" (Luke 19:10, RSV). As those who represent him today, we have no greater task ourselves.

3
God's Way into Our Lives

Acts 17:16–34

"He Is Not Far From . . . Us"

God did not give us a caretaker's job when he put the gospel into our hands. To keep the church in smooth running order, to keep our traditions dusted and polished, or to keep a watchful eye on our family and special friends is not our main job. These things we must do. But he gave us a far bigger task. The world, with its triumphs and its despairs, its beauty and its ugliness, has moved next door to every one of us. Each day hurls new challenges at our faith.

This was true as long ago as the time of the apostle Paul. If Paul had limited his interests and concern to the Jews, his work would have been far simpler. No one had to tell him how Jews thought. He knew their Scriptures; he knew their traditions; he spoke their language. He was a Jew himself. But God flung him out into an intellectual wilderness where he had to forage in strange places for food for his Gentile audiences. Walking among the Greek philosophers, he found a scrap here and there which looked remarkably like the bread on which he had lived as a Jew. But the Greeks called him a "babbler"—a "seed-picker"— one who gathers up and gives out odd bits of the thoughts of others. Even so, he stuck out his neck and let them have their laughs. For his trouble he won a few people to Jesus Christ.

Today all sorts of ideas swirl about us like autumn leaves in a dust devil; the faces of people blur like the figures standing on a subway platform as we ride by; prayers lose themselves in the cries of the marketplace. And we find ourselves, the aspiring creators of a better world, trying to bring a semblance of order out of the chaos of the times.

I

Wouldn't it be much easier for us if we could be absolutely sure that God is at work in all mankind? Yet we are overwhelmed by the hurricane force of the demonic. It is often far easier to see Satan's hand than God's hand in the world, especially if we live where this hurricane force has struck again and again. Nations and factions will not quit fighting each other; the strong crush the weak; murder stalks the streets; charge and countercharge fly back and forth in the heat of political rivalry.

Nevertheless, God is at work. In a passage that catalogs some of the worst varieties of human evil, Paul wrote even of the wicked: "For what can be known about God is plain to them, because God has shown it to them. Ever since the creation of the world his invisible nature, namely, his eternal power and deity, has been clearly perceived in the things that have been made" (Rom. 1:19-20, RSV). God has revealed himself in his creation both by what he has made and by what he continues to do. No one can escape this revelation.

But it is not just the power of the sunset, the majesty of the universe, or the awesomeness of the unknown that moves men to recognize God. We have to do also with the work of his wrath. He makes himself known in anger and indignation. When idolatry has its innings and is out, when man reaps the harvest of his wrongdoing, when the universe impresses itself upon us as a moral universe, then we feel, "Surely God is at work!" And it makes sense. If God were not at work, how could we account for the prophet who rises out of the moral shambles of his times, declaring, "God commands all men to repent"?

It is true, God seeks us—but we are seeking after God, too. We sometimes hotly deny it; we flee at the sound of his name;

we try to hide from him among the things he has made, but in
some way or other we want him. We pour out our ambitions
and our passions upon a thousand altars—wealth, position, power,
pleasure, and security in all their forms—and yet within our hearts
we erect a secret altar to the unknown God. We run from God
only to stumble into his arms.

Or we actively and consciously seek God, like Charles Haddon
Spurgeon, the famous preacher of the past century, who as a
teenage lad wandered from church to church trying to find a
merciful and forgiving God; or like the brilliant youth with the
highest ethical code, who lingered after class with his philosophy
professor, pressing him for reasons for believing in God.

As the apostle put it, God has so made men "that they should
seek God, in the hope that they might feel after him and find
him. Yet he is not far from each one of us, for 'In him we live
and move and have our being'" (Acts 17:27–28, RSV). This is
the fact that looses upon us an avalanche of responsibility. Perhaps we ask, "What can we do?"

II

We can do several things.

For one thing, we can face the world and try, at least, to look
every man in the eye. That in itself is a sort of victory, for we
find it easy enough to steer clear of any situation that would
make us uncomfortable or put us on the defensive with our faith.
One encounter with an icily skeptical and critical person, and
we are tempted to retreat to some cozy sanctuary, lick our wounds,
and comfort ourselves with the promises of Christ to the persecuted.

Some interpreters think Paul did that: that he left Athens with
a red face and downcast eyes, determined that from then on he
would stick to his own ways of thinking and understanding and
not dabble in the philosophical conceits of the Epicureans and

Stoics. This might be so. Paul might have had excellent personal reasons for doing so; but this would not decide what you and I should do in a similar situation. Besides, I am not convinced that this is the last time Paul used his Areopagus tactics. Didn't he write to the Corinthian church, "For though I am free from all men, I have made myself a slave to all, that I might win the more. I have become all things to all men, that I might by all means save some" (1 Cor. 9:19,22, RSV)? But we have to admit it is easier for most of us to avoid situations where we might be challenged and where there is a strong likelihood of failure.

If God is at work among all men, you and I don't have a one-sided selling job to do. Spiritual arm-twisting is neither permissible nor necessary. There is no room in Christian witnessing for the canned answer and the engineered decision. There is plenty of room for the kind of courage and honesty that makes a man as quick to say, "I don't know" as to say, "I know whom I have believed." The monolithic, impersonal, "I'm right—you're wrong" approach to the unbeliever is deadly, even if we're right. Therefore, the way of friendly exchange and of positive witness is open to us provided we truly care about persons as persons and not as statistics.

Somehow we will have to find a point of contact with the people of our time. We have many things in common with our neighbors and with the people who work beside us: sports, the arts, government, books, and travel; home, children, food, taxes, and our aches and pains. But by point of contact I mean something deeper. When Paul walked among the Athenians, he was able, after the first heat of his anger at the idols had died down, to reconsider the religious beliefs of the Athenians for what they were worth. He cut through to the basic matter of what they believed, what they aspired to, and what they actually needed. He saw that the people before him had religious aspirations, just as he did, and openly acknowledged it. Then he went down the

line with beliefs that he held in common with them. Because
he started where they were, because he did not demand that
they begin where he was, they listened.

We do not have to go far to discover how men live from day
to day: what makes them swear, what keeps them awake at night,
what makes the future look like a blind alley. We hear modern
man saying such things as:

> "Life doesn't add up to anything."
> "I don't really mean anything to anybody—
>   I'm just a statistic."
> "I wish I could be sure of something."
> "This world is run either by a devil or a lunatic."
> "I wish somebody could tell me what is right
>   and what is wrong."[1]

Start talking with a man about the widespread feeling of the
meaninglessness of existence, the depersonalization of our lives,
the abyss of insecurity that undermines every certainty, the demonic in human affairs, and the ambiguities of ethical behavior,
and right away you will have an audience. You will be talking
about *him,* reading his secret sorrow, probing his pain and confu-
sion, and in the process opening wellsprings of understanding.
We ought not to be alarmed when we come up against skepticism
and unbelief in the modern world: it only shows us our task in
bold relief. Paul Tillich reminded us that the despair of our times
reflected in much of modern art and drama poses the questions
that it is the business of the Christian faith to answer. Any man's
doubt is faith's opportunity.

III

It ought to be clear that a great duty is laid upon us in these
days, a duty to attempt to lead men to a transforming experience
of God, requiring us to prepare ourselves as Christian believers
to do the job. We can see also that this is not a task to handle

through our own wisdom and cunning. And we do not have to. Why?

Well, God has taken it upon himself to come to man, to break into history in such a way that we can take hold of him, to assume the burden of our ignorance and weakness and come in person to give us truth and power. Paul could go only so far with the Athenians on their own terms. There was a gap between the revelation of God in nature and the revelation of God in Jesus Christ. The world and the philosopher could tell some things about God, but not everything. God himself had to come and finish the story and show its meaning. And that is precisely what he did when Christ came. So men do not have to look until their eyes are red-rimmed, trying to see what the heavens say about God. Men do not have to fish around in their own minds to find the answer to the mystery of God. What men could never do, God himself has done. He has revealed what we could never discover. Christ the living Lord is in the world: he is God's response to man's groping hand that fingers the brooding mystery of the heavens.

Does this mean that when we present this Christ to the world with more expertise all our worries will be over, that men will be overwhelmed by the power of this revealed truth? Hardly. It did not happen when men stood face-to-face with Christ, when they saw his signs, when they heard his teaching, or when they heard the story of the resurrection. To some, Christ is a stumbling-block; to others, foolishness. When Paul finished his sermon in the Areopagus, where he had presented Christ in no uncertain terms, some mocked. So acceptance is not guaranteed. However, others wanted to hear more and a few believed. Therefore, "to those who are called, . . . Christ [is] the power of God and the wisdom of God" (1 Cor. 1:24, RSV).

This revelation of God in Christ stands forever as God's way of getting at our hearts with his judgment and his mercy. And going right along with it, and absolutely necessary to it, is the work of the Holy Spirit. The Holy Spirit takes the event that happened two thousand years ago and makes it real and effective in lives today. When we bear our Christian witness, the God who raised Jesus Christ from the dead offers life to the dead spirits of those who hear us. Some of the best work of the Holy Spirit goes on after we have said good-bye and closed the door behind us, leaving a soul to his own thoughts. C. S. Lewis gave this account of his conversion: "You must picture me," he writes, "alone in that room in Magdalen, night after night, feeling, whenever my mind lifted even for a second from my work, the steady, unrelenting approach of Him whom I so earnestly desired not to meet." [2] This is why we dare believe that if we do not neglect our opportunities to give an intelligent, sincere testimony to the meaning of our faith, God can make every word we say weigh a ton.

The conclusion of this entire matter is this: the measurable results of our work may be disappointing, but we shall not fail if we are faithful to our task and accept God's standards of success. It was not an impressive number of disciples that followed Paul from the Areopagus, but there was one among them, who, we are told, later became the respected bishop of Athens and whose writings inspired hundreds through the centuries, Dionysius the Areopagite. None of us can measure the far-reaching effectiveness of our work for Christ, for the gospel "is the power of God for salvation to every one who has faith, to the Jew first and also to the Greek" (Rom. 1:16, RSV).

[1] Compare H. H. Farmer, *The Servant of the Word* (Philadelphia: Fortress Press, 1942), pp. 89–109.
[2] C. S. Lewis, *Surprised by Joy* (New York: Harcourt, Brace and Company, 1955), p. 228.

4
Your Right to God's Promises

2 Peter 1:1–11

"What He Has Promised Us, Eternal Life"

When a cousin of mine was a small boy, a schoolmate invited him to his birthday party on the following Saturday afternoon. My cousin burst into the house after school that afternoon and proudly announced to his mother that he had been invited to a birthday party. His parents were delighted too, for the birthday boy was from one of the finest homes in town. The next day the family drove several miles to a nearby town and bought my cousin a new suit and a present to give his schoolmate. Saturday afternoon came, and my uncle let my cousin out of the car and drove off. My cousin went to the door wearing his brand-new suit and happily carrying the birthday present and rang the doorbell and waited. No one came to the door. He rang again. Still no one came. After waiting several minutes and hearing no signs of life in the house, he concluded that there was a mistake and went home in tears. Actually, there was no mistake at all—my cousin's classmate wouldn't have a birthday for six months. If ever the saying "all dressed up and no place to go" applied, it applied to my cousin.

Our profoundest disappointments come, not because hopes that we have projected in fantasy have failed to come to fruition, but because promises freely made have not been fulfilled. It is bad enough to wish for something and work for it but never achieve it. How much more poignant to trustingly expect something that has been promised only to have one's faith shattered.

A few years ago a graduate student wrote a doctoral dissertation

31

dealing with the problem "why church members drop out." After talking with numerous dropouts, he discovered that their loss of interest in the church often followed disenchantment with the ministers' promises that were freely given but not fulfilled. In a counseling session or during a home visit the minister, aware of some problem troubling his parishioner, would promise to visit and talk with a person or to deal with some specific problem, only to forget about it.

What of God's promises? In the New Testament two particular Greek words are used more than fifty times to speak of the promises of God. These same two words, both as verb and noun, appeared in classical Greek and were used in several ways. William Barclay has pointed out that these words translated as "promise" in the New Testament were used in classical Greek to refer to public announcements, such as announcements of festivals or games; to refer to a promise freely offered and volunteered; also, to project an image, such as making political promises in campaigns; in offering, as the Sophist philosophers did, to teach anything for pay; in a lover's professions of love for someone; in claims for curative properties of certain drugs.[1] There was always the possibility of the promise's failure in fulfillment. We well know, for example, that political promises are not always kept, that a lover's promises are often a pretense, that claims made for products of many kinds are frequently exaggerated.

What of God's promises as compared to man's? The apostle Paul said, "God must be true, even though every man is a liar" (Rom. 3:4, TEV).

Nothing could be more relevant to our needs today than an awareness of God's promises. Because of the destructiveness of sin, because of the apparent injustice of human suffering, and because of the apparent finality of death, we need to know what God has promised about them all. I want to assert that the promise of God stands in opposition to every negative force in the universe and in opposition to every negative force operating in the individual life.

I

Remember, it is *God* who promises.

What was it that sustained the Jewish people through the centuries of their dramatic, often tragic history? It was the promises of God, such as the promise of God to Abraham, as recorded in the twelfth chapter of Genesis: "And I will make of you a great nation, and I will bless you, and make your name great, so that you will be a blessing. I will bless those who bless you, and him who curses you I will curse; and by you all the families of the earth shall bless themselves" (Gen. 12:2–3, RSV).

In 1963 I made my first visit to New York City. I arrived by taxi at Hastings Hall of the Union Theological Seminary, where I was to stay during a few weeks of study, and deposited my bags. Then I went outside and walked past the Riverside Church and across the street, where I stood and looked for a while at the interesting sights across the Hudson River. As I walked back to my room, I looked across the street at the Jewish Theological Seminary and saw something that struck me more forcefully than the Riverside Church or the view across the Hudson River. On the front of the building was a sculpture of the burning bush and an inscription: "The bush burned and it was not consumed." I was struck by that sculpture and that inscription because in them was wrapped up the key to the courage and survival of the Jewish people. The presence and power of God in all of the holocausts of history enabled them to endure. God had promised; they believed God's promise; and that was that!

During his presidential campaign, President Carter said to the American people, "I will never lie to you." Any man, theoretically, can say, "I will never lie to you." No man, however, can truthfully say, "I *cannot* lie to you," for it can be said only of God, that he cannot lie. Remember, therefore, that when we are talking about the promises of God that it is God who cannot lie who has promised.

What has God promised?

II

What God has promised is essentially eternal life, that is, participation in the life of God himself. John tells us that what is promised to us is eternal life (1 John 2:25).

Eternal life does not mean exactly what we might assume on first hearing the words. Eternal life is a quality of life, rather than life that merely stretches out endlessly. As our Lord prayed in his intercessory prayer, he defined the meaning in these words: "And this is eternal life, that they know thee the only true God, and Jesus Christ whom thou hast sent" (John 17:3, RSV). In ancient Greek mythology, there is a story that will help us to understand the difference between eternal life thought of as a mere quantity and eternal life in its qualitative meaning. In this story, Aurora, the goddess of the dawn, fell in love with Tithonus, the mortal youth. Zeus, the supreme God, offered her any gift that she might choose for her mortal lover. She asked that Tithonus might have immortality, but she forgot to ask that he might always have youth and vigor. So Tithonus lived on and on and grew more and more decrepit, until life became unbearable.

When God gives us eternal life, he gives us not just eternal existence, he gives us *meaningful* eternal existence in himself!

When does this eternal life begin?

III

Eternal life is entered into *now*.

The good things that God has for us are not all in some nebulous, far-off future. God wants us to know him here in this life, and he makes it possible for us to know something of himself now. This is described in a beautiful text in Paul's first letter to the Corinthians, a text often incorrectly applied to heaven. "'What no eye has seen, nor ear heard,/ nor the heart of man conceived,/ what God has prepared for those who love him,'/ God has revealed to us through the Spirit" (2:9–10, RSV).

The words that the circus barker cries, "This is only the beginning, folks! This is only the beginning!" are words that apply to our experience of God in *this* life: indeed, it is only the beginning, like the acorn as compared with the full-grown oak.

Where does this eternal life, this life of God himself, touch down in our human experience?

IV

This promise of eternal life, as I have defined it, penetrates every area of our human existence.

The promise of eternal life is the solution for the problem of our sin. Consider the words of John: "Beloved, we are God's children now; it does not appear what we shall be, but we know that when he appears we shall be like him, for we shall see him as he is. And every one who thus hopes in him purifies himself as he is pure" (1 John 3:2–3, RSV).

The promise of eternal life is also the solution for the problem of human suffering. Walter Lippmann, the philosopher-journalist, wrote, "The greatest of all perplexities in theology has been to reconcile the infinite goodness of God with his omnipotence." Suffering is indeed the perennial problem, but some have gained a victory in spite of it.

Suffering was a problem for the ancient Job, but he was able through his confidence in God to say, "Though he slay me, yet will I trust in him" (Job 13:15). Suffering was a problem for the author, Robert Louis Stevenson, but he was able to say, "I believe in an ultimate decency of things; ay, and if I woke in hell, should still believe it!"

The promise of eternal life is, moreover, the solution for the problem of death. The resurrection of our Lord Jesus Christ was God's reaffirmation of his promise of life, which had stood over so many generations of human history.

But why would God make such promises to us?

V

It should be clear to us that the promise was not made because of anything good or worthy that we have done or that we could possibly do.

God's promise was freely given, born of his love. The final purpose of the promise is to do good. It is not the intention of God to take away from us anything that is good for us. What a regrettable mistake some people make about God and religion and morals. Somewhere they acquire the idea that God is determined to rob us of something worthwhile, something that would make us happy. To the contrary, God would take away or conquer those things that harm us. The apostle Peter says that the purpose of the promise is, for one thing, to enable us to "escape from the corruption that is in the world" (v. 4, RSV). That is to say, God wants us to be freed from our fixations on idols, on those things within ourselves or about us that would keep us enslaved to this world and its sights and sounds and feelings and aspirations. A second purpose, and related to the first, is to enable us to become "partakers of the divine nature." God wants us to know something of himself, of his life, of his purposes, even while we live in this world, where it is so easy to forget those things that are above, where Christ is seated at the right hand of God.

How, then, does the promise become effective in your life and mine?

VI

We enter into the blessings of God's promise through faith and works.

We enjoy some blessings of God regardless of faith and works. Jesus said that God makes the sun to shine on the good and the bad alike. You don't have to be a Christian, or a praying person, to enjoy many of the blessings of God.

However, the fullness of the promise of God belongs only to those who receive it consciously and deliberately. One writer suggests this comparison. A father promises his son a college education. It is the father's genuine intention to see that his son gets a college education. The father is confident that he can carry out his promise, for he has the material resources to underwrite the promise. However, the son may never get a college education, not because the father has not promised it, not because the father is unwilling or unable to carry out his promise, but because the son does not avail himself of the promise that his father has made.[2] So it is with God's promise of eternal life, with all of the abundance, the richness that this implies: we have to enter into it, receive it by faith, and let it begin its good work in us, giving us new aims, new desires, new joys, new ways of using our energies, new ways of relating ourselves to the people with whom we live.

This promise of eternal life is inescapable. We may ignore it; we may run from it; we may fight to rid ourselves of it. Nevertheless, the promise meets us around every corner of our life. It is there, for God is there, and always to do us good. How we need to stop and consider and feel and rejoice! The music of Finlandia brings to my mind the haunting words of Katharina von Schlegel that I heard our college choir sing so movingly when I was a college freshman:

> Be still, my soul: the Lord is on thy side;
>   Bear patiently the cross of grief or pain;
> Leave to thy God to order and provide;
>   In every change He faithful will remain.

The promise is there, just where you are even now. You may not recognize it, but it is there because God loves you and he wants your life not only to last forever, but to be abundant and meaningful now *and* everlastingly.

> Be still, my soul: thy best, thy heavenly
>   Friend,
> Thro' thorny ways leads to a joyful end.

[1] William Barclay, *More New Testament Words* (London: SMC Press, Ltd., 1958), pp. 57–58.

[2] Cf. Barclay, ibid., pp. 59–60.

5
Ship of Fools

Matthew 8:18–27, RSV

"When He Got into the Boat, His Disciples Followed"

When Katherine Anne Porter published her long-awaited novel, *Ship of Fools,* she explained why she had borrowed the title from a fifteenth-century moral allegory: "I took for my own this simple almost universal image of the ship of this world on its voyage to eternity . . . I am a passenger on that ship."

We, too, are passengers on a ship. Shall we call it a ship of fools? Let us hope that we are, as Paul phrased, it, "fools for Christ's sake" (1 Cor. 4:10). When he twice used the word *mōros* (fool) he had discipleship in mind, like Matthew when he told the story of the stilling of the tempest.

In what ways are we Christians, church people, a ship of fools, though it be fools for Christ's sake?

I

To begin with, if we take our discipleship seriously we have to renounce the usual securities. For two men, Jesus' orders to go across to the eastern shore of the Sea of Galilee meant just that, to renounce the usual securities. They did not think so, and they had their glib confessions and excuses handy when the challenge came to them.

"Teacher," one of them said, "I will follow you wherever you go." Knowing you is the greatest privilege of life! I can think of nothing more delightful than to go wherever you go and have a part in your great work! Such a man thinks of thousand-voice choirs and persons stumbling over one another to fill a stadium to hear his hero preach. The other man in the story said, "Lord, let me first go and bury my father." I would do nothing to bring pain to my loved ones! The commandment to honor father and mother I take seriously! When everything is tidied up at home, I'll be completely free! Then I can follow you without distraction! So went the responses when Jesus cried, "All aboard!"

Our Lord made it crystal clear that the future holds no guarantee of comfort for anyone who follows him: "Foxes have holes, and birds of the air have nests; but the Son of man has nowhere to lay his head." When Bonhoeffer declared that the call to discipleship is a call to die, he declared against "cheap grace." He did not have in mind sure and certain martyrdom, a suicide mission for all the faithful. Yet that call is a summons to die daily, to share in the suffering of Christ, to live a style of life in which literal death is a possibility.

Jesus also made it clear that the past provides no absolute precedents for anyone who follows him: "Follow me, and leave the dead to bury their own dead." Morality as usual must step back when the Lord of the sabbath steps up. It is perfectly possible for any of us so to box ourselves in with the precepts and precedents of the past that we cannot go anywhere. Some of the situation ethicists may have been wrong on certain points, as when we were led to believe that we have to start from scratch whenever we make a moral judgment. But they were right in reminding us that the patterns of the past cannot show us all that we need to know about serving God.

II

The fact is, instead of enjoying security with its cozy comforts and its time-honored guidelines, we are flung out into storms that threaten our very existence.

To follow Jesus Christ means to go with him into the very teeth of the storm. The first few steps seem simple and harmless enough. The sky is clear, the sun is shining, the wind is gentle. "And when he got into the boat, his disciples followed him." It is as natural as that, no fuss, no flurry of excitement at the office, no change of pattern in the routine of life. Smooth sailing is the order of the day! And then the storm!

The storm! For the disciples with Jesus it was one of those well-known tempests that sometimes struck fishermen on the Sea of Galilee when they hardly expected it. For us, the storm may be the critical illness of a child, the embarrassing loss of a job, conflict in the home, temptation to some kind of wrongdoing, or a collapse of religious faith. It may also be a nation in crisis or a world on the verge of war. For a mother whose child was dying of an incurable illness, novelist Peter DeVries saw it like this: "Suddenly she gave in to a burst of rage. She cursed and blasphemed, reviling the name of God and all the members of the Trinity individually. She heaped abuse upon the mother of Christ, in a language so obscene that she later recoiled in horror from the memory of it." So the storm may arise in the ordinary course of life. Life is like that. Nobody escapes suffering, humiliation, conflict, temptation, doubt, or fear. For some it is mild; for others, catastrophic.

It can be an unnerving prospect, letting ourselves in for the descent of the storm and all that goes with it. Sometimes we are psychologically prepared for it; sometimes not. Like Uncle Remus' Br'er Rabbit, who was "born and bred in the brierpatch," we may be tough-minded enough through early conditioning to take what comes with passable aplomb. But most of the time we are like the disciples; terrified by what is happening and by what we fear is about to happen. This was no ordinary storm, and if the disciples ever had a right to their terror it was then. Matthew uses a term to describe the fierceness of the storm which puts it into a special class: "a great earthquake (a great shaking) in the sea."

How descriptive this may be of what happens in your life and mine! All is peaceful; the wind is just stiff enough to give tone and vitality to life; gaiety and good fellowship abound. And suddenly out of nowhere comes the storm! The embarrassing headline in the morning newspaper, the stabbing pain in the chest in the middle of the night, the ominous long-distance call reporting an accident, the notice from your employer that your services are no longer needed—any one of these events may be enough to turn a wonderful day or year or lifetime inside out and do it in less than a minute.

The storm always threatens to destroy us: a storm of Matthean dimensions produces a real crisis. In the Chinese language, two characters stand for the word *crisis,* one of them picturing danger and the other, opportunity. Opportunity, yes, but always danger! It has been said that one earthquake many years ago, in which many thousands were killed, produced more atheists than all the arguments of the unbelievers of all time. The unsettling, catastrophic experiences of life make God seem unaware or uncaring. Why was Jesus asleep when the disciples needed him most? Why does God wait in chilly silence when incredible events are breaking furiously about us? "Save, Lord; we are perishing" (v. 25, RSV), we cry, and wonder why it is necessary to cry at all.

III

Our old securities fail us, our new uncharted experiences threaten to overwhelm us, and then we discover our true security.

Trouble drives us to pray as we have never prayed before. Of course, the *way* we pray sometimes suggests our little faith. We pray as if the God of heaven himself, like Baal, is asleep and has to be wheedled or pressured into noticing our plight. But the Old Testament teaches us that the silence of the sabbath is important, as well as the activity of the remainder of the week. God is present; God keeps his universe intact while he observes the sabbath. The Father was never closer to the Son, the Father was never doing a greater thing than when the silence of heaven caused Jesus to cry out from the cross, "My God, my God, why hast thou forsaken me?" (Matt. 27:46). When the disciples were embattled on the sea, the sleeping Lord was the calm in the eye of the storm, and they did not know it. When we fret and beg and thrash about in our doubt and discomfort, fearing that utter disaster has struck and that we cannot survive and that heaven is unconcerned, even then—and especially then—our Lord is present: "Closer is He than breathing, and nearer than hands and feet." Once the colorful Methodist Bishop Quayle walked the floor with a problem far into the night until he heard God speak to him: "Quayle, you go to bed. I'll sit up the rest of the night."

To come frantically to God, pounding on the gate of heaven, may not be the best faith, but it is faith, and far better than no faith at all. It is probably all that most of us can summon at any time. Perhaps Christ says to us, as to the men in the ship, "Why are you afraid, O men of little faith?" But we are men of faith for all that!

If we manage to get out our bungling prayers, if we are at last assured that God knows and cares what happens to us, if we stand waiting and expectant that he will do what is best, then surely something significant will happen.

Perhaps the Lord will quell the storm of seismic events which threatens our existence. Matthew is telling us that God as he was known in Jesus Christ is in ultimate control of the most formidable forces there are, that God is the conqueror of the first and last enemy of man, and that we should not be astonished at anything God might do. If he can tame the wild storm, he can raise up the sick, he can give you a better job than the one you lost, he can bring peace to a troubled family or world, he can break the back of temptation, and he can bring strength and radiance once more to a jaded faith.

To still the tempest outside may not, however, be his greatest favor. That may be his quelling of the storm within our hearts. The child may die, you may never get another job as good as the one you lost, the divorce may go through, national problems may drag on and on unsolved, temptation may harass you incessantly, and unbelief, like a vulture, may sit menacingly on the horizon of your daily life. Yet, all is well, for the Lord of the tempest acts: he rebukes the wind and the sea of your fears and makes a great calm.

Faith is real when we can accept his answer to our prayers any way he chooses to give it, like the father who cried out to his three sons above the fury of a storm at sea, "Living or dying God saves his own child." "At twilight," said Alistair MacLean in *High Country*, "four silent men came to harbor. In their hearts was the hush of a great awe." When Christ has dealt with us and the winds and the sea are at rest, we will find ourselves saying with the first disciples, "What sort of man is this, that even winds and sea obey him?" knowing that the ancient story is true because we have seen it happen all over again when it happened to us.

Were we fools to get into the ship? Perhaps! But fools for Christ's sake, for the sake of others, and for our own sake. You see, God is there with us. And that makes the difference!

6
What Love Requires

Galatians 6:1–5,9–10, RSV

"Bear One Another's Burdens"

A writer in a St. Louis newspaper said, "Everybody in business should own a basset hound. Then when you come home at night, your dog will always look like he has more problems than you have." All of us know what he meant, for all of us have problems, troubles, burdens.

You can identify three types of burdens that we and others about us carry. First, the unnecessary burdens. These come to us because we act in stupidity—moral and practical stupidity. A little bit of forethought or a little bit of moral courage would have spared us. Next, the inevitable burdens. These come to us through no fault of our own. Sometimes it is the fault of a very selfish or a criminal person; sometimes we can blame no one at all—accidents do happen. Then, the voluntary burdens. We pick them up not because we are stupid or cowardly, not because we can't avoid them, but because we must . . . because it is "the law of Christ" . . . because we care.[1]

Too often we have spoken of love and interpreted it negatively. We have measured it by the scope of our willingness to deny ourselves, how much we are willing to give up for others. And this can be pretty depressing. We don't come off too well.

But Paul puts love within reach. It is something we can do today, this very day in this year of our Lord. He says, "Bear one another's burdens, and so fulfil the law of Christ."

Perhaps the need to do this sort of thing is greater than most of us are aware of. Some fellow student may be about to lose

his spiritual and moral capital by gambling with his private interpretation of situation ethics. He needs caring for. A student wife
and mother may be crushed or bruised by a series of events that
she could not prevent. She needs caring for. A professor may
be overextending himself as he goes beyond the call of duty in
trying to be of help to his students. He needs caring for.

These needs indicate some of the kinds of things we can do
for one another. At the same time they represent opportunities
to experience what it means to be truly human, to be a part of
a community that cares.

What are some of the principles that should guide us in trying
to fulfill what Paul calls "the law of Christ"?

I

First, we need to recognize one another's personhood—and personhood includes at its very heart both freedom and responsibility.

Paul tells us, "Each man will have to bear his own load." Some
things no man can avoid. Some things we can't shift to another's
shoulders. Have you ever wished so deeply that a friend of yours
would accept and follow the Christ you love, that you would
gladly make his decision for him? Yet you know that it is impossible. The most important decisions of our lives are as individual
as our own fingerprints. I can't decide them for you. You can't
decide them for me.

Sometimes we like to blame others for our troubles. An alco-
holic blames his father or his grandfather, thinking that this lets
him off the hook. Many of us may blame Adam or the devil.
How convenient! Some years ago in Germany I picked up a magazine whose cover told an eloquent and bitter story without a
word. Standing in the midst of the rubble of an earthquake, a
man shook his fist toward heaven. Some people blame God for
their troubles. But will this work?

Studdert-Kennedy, the colorful chaplain of World War I, put the issue sharply when he said that when he stood before the eternal judgment seat he expected God to ask him but one question: Well, what did you make of it? [2]

II

In the second place, having decided that there are some things we cannot do for others, we need to go on to learn what we can do.

Of course, we can be too eager to help, like the Boy Scout who got into a fight with a little old lady who didn't want to cross the street.

But that may not be our problem. Do we prefer not to know what the needs of others are, so that we cannot be expected to help? The story of Dives, as Helmut Thielicke has graphically shown, may be the story of your attitude. The rich man closed his eyes when his carriage passed through the slums. He drew the curtains at home so that the sight of some wretched creature will not incite his pity. Lazarus lay at his back door every day, but Dives never saw him.

Nevertheless, life will not let us alone. Life shatters our cleverest defenses. Sooner or later life lets us know how things are. Your close friend gets in some kind of trouble. Your father or brother loses his job. Your wife becomes seriously ill. Then you know what it is to be human. "Deep calls unto deep," and you cannot avoid the cry.

For one reason or another, you may find yourself in a kind of hell on earth and wonder why God put you there. As Christoph Blumhardt observed, perchance you are the only person available to represent him adequately in that area of hell. Alcoholics Anonymous has demonstrated that some experiences uniquely prepare one to help people with burdens peculiar to those experiences.

We have only to look about us, keep our spiritual radar tuned in, and go about our work. Our eyes, our ears, and our hearts will tell us where there is need.

III

In the third place, as we learn of what we can do for someone, we need to recognize our own vulnerability.

Paul warned, "Look to yourself, lest you too be tempted." Good advice! Why?

Well, it is easy to take a lofty attitude toward others, to be patronizing, condescending. In saving a sinner, I may become a worse sinner. I may become guilty of what Henry Drummond called "sins of the temper."

On the other hand, I may grow so sympathetic with a man "overtaken in [a] trespass" that I join him in what brought on his troubles. A biographer of a popular nineteenth-century preacher said of him that the preacher's approach to a vice was first to denounce it, then to acknowledge its possible merits, and finally to practice it.

Still, if we fulfill the law of Christ, if we bear one another's burdens, we have to take the risks, and they are considerable.

IV

In the fourth place, in order to approach and respond to other persons in the right spirit, we need to let others help us with our own burdens.

Our fellowmen can help us. Jesus knew that. Even he found comfort and strength in his disciples and in his friends, Mary, Martha, and Lazarus. In Albert Camus' book, *The Plague,* the author draws a picture of a priest named Paneloux who in one scene denounces the people of Oran, charging that the plague among them is the judgment of God upon them for their sins. "You . . . you . . . you," he cries in accusation. Days later, the priest saw a little boy die. Even in suffering and death, the innocent child unknowingly ministered to the priest, lifting his burden of arrogance and self-righteousness. After that, Paneloux climbed into his pulpit again. This time, his manner was different. "He spoke in a gentler, more thoughtful tone than on the previous occasion, and several times was noticed to be stumbling over his words. A yet more noteworthy change was that instead of saying 'you' he now said 'we.' "

Furthermore, we must remember that our Lord himself can help us. Before Jesus' disciples went into the world with his message, they had to heed his words: "You are [my] witnesses . . . ; but stay in the city, until you are clothed with power from on high" (Luke 24:48–49, RSV).

Several years ago when Dr. Robert J. McCracken, then minister of Riverside Church, gave the Mullins Lectures, a friend related a fact that deeply impressed me. He had once roomed with Dr. McCracken at a meeting and observed that Dr. McCracken each night got down on his knees, like a Junior boy, at his bedside and said his prayers. Dr. McCracken knew where he needed to go, as a human being, as a Christian, and as a minister of Christ to receive his help. So it was no surprise to me to read later, in one of his sermons: "And if you are confused in mind, or bewildered by doubt, or if you have fallen into sin, and still long to find God, do something very simple, so simple that we all forget its efficacy. Get down on your knees, wait till all the voices in your heart are still, and then say, 'Our Father, who art in heaven . . .' "

Now we come back to where we started. "Bear one another's burdens, and so fulfil the law of Christ."

Though it isn't the most important reason for doing so, to help a fellowman bear his burdens will do something wonderful for you. Someone has said, "The entire sum of existence is the magic of being needed by just one person."

The most compelling reason is this: What you do about the burdens of a fellowman may be decisive—utterly decisive—for him. Lord Shaftesbury, I am told, once walked up to a man who was being released from prison for the nineteenth time, shook hands with him, and said, "Ah, Maynard, we'll make a man of you yet. We'll make a man of you yet." The man testified, years later, as he recalled the incident, "That was forty-three years ago come Michaelmas and I've never seen the inside of a prison cell since."

The range of our caring begins, of course, with the persons nearest to us, but it extends to the community that surrounds us, and even to generations yet unborn, so that even air pollution, the population explosion, and war become our proper burdens. For we are challenged by the "breadth and length and height and depth" (Eph. 3:18, RSV) of the love of Christ.

[1] Compare Oscar Blackwelder, *The Interpreter's Bible* (New York: Abingdon Press, 1953), Vol. X, pp. 577–78.

[2] As cited by Harry Emerson Fosdick, *A Great Time to Be Alive* (New York: Harper and Brothers, 1944), p. 53. Cf. G. A. Studdert-Kennedy, "Well?" *The Sorrows of God and Other Poems* (New York: George H. Doran Company, 1924), pp. 127–32.

7

Religion as a Form and a Force

2 Timothy 3:5

"Holding the Form . . . Denying the Power"

I

The apostle speaks of "men who preserve the outward form of religion, but are a standing denial of its reality" (2 Tim. 3:5, NEB).

This kind of statement makes sensitive, sincere Christians a bit anxious. We believe we want to take our religion seriously, to let it be more than a mere form in our lives, to allow it to make us more useful people in the world. But we can't be sure. We look at ourselves and see much that is either wrong or lacking. Sometimes we feel more like going fishing than going to church. And we may even at times feel more like cursing than praying.

But that is not what bothers us most of the time. Sooner or later, the average Christian comes to terms with his humanity. He recognizes and accepts his lack of perfection. He allows for his vagrant feelings. What bothers us most, or ought to bother us, is that the church as a whole is making such a little dent in the armor plate of secularism and materialism. We have vast resources of personnel, of money, and of tradition, and yet we are weak. No group can beat us at the game of social commentary, analysis, and diagnosis. We even claim that we have the remedy for what ails the world. Yet many of the aims of Christians through the ages seem so far from realization: peace, justice, and personal righteousness. One pastor expressed his bitterness about a member of his church: "That man," the pastor said, "is so

51

crooked that when he dies we won't bury him: we'll just twist
him into the ground."

II

Perhaps that's good enough for the crooked man who has
walked the last crooked mile. What about the rest of us? What
is wrong with us? Let's try to keep matters in proper perspective.
There has always been something wrong with the church. Some
of us keep hoping that we will break out of our bondage and
be truly free. Perhaps that hope has kept the church in business
through the centuries. But we'll have to acknowledge that we've
done more talking than doing; that we've kept our ecclesiastical
machinery purring smoothly and haven't paid enough attention
to what it is producing. We have brought people off the assembly
line "who preserve the outward form of religion, but are a standing denial of its reality."

God knows that the world needs what religion has promised
so beautifully or called for so insistently. But repeated disappointment has made some persons raise serious questions about the
whole religious enterprise—whether to throw it away entirely
or to do some other drastic thing with it. What should we do?

III

We can go at the problem in any of several ways.

We might reject religion entirely. This is one possibility. But
it is out of keeping with what seems to be a natural inclination
of most of mankind. It goes against the traditions of our own
nation. And it probably would be psychologically traumatic to
us individually.

Yet it becomes easier and easier to get rid of religion—at least
what is conventionally called religion—by soaking up arguments
so freely disseminated today; by riding the crest of the waves
of rebellion sweeping the modern world; or by assuming that

something as old as religion can't be relevant and worthwhile. I would be really surprised not to find at least a few persons who are on the verge of tossing the old faith through the stained glass window.

One of the greatest preachers of America wrote his mother from college when he was a student, saying, "I'm going to clear God out of the universe, start all over, and see where I come out." It is easier than it once was to reject religion: you can find some social approval for your action, and you may be paid handsomely to speak or write on your views. Still you have to deal with yourself and with all that lies deep within you. For example, a client of psychologist Carl Rogers, trying to dimiss his guilt and the somatic symptoms that went along with it, said, "Intellectually I'm a pagan, but I'm a Puritan in my guts." To reject religion entirely is hard to do.

We might do something else. We might simply reject the form of religion. Some persons are unhappy that the church has become a political forum—a place for a lot of talk and little effective action. The church, they say, is trying to do things, even good things, that it is not always qualified to do. But mostly there is talk, divisive talk, and largely ineffectual action.

Some years ago, according to *Time* magazine, Ralph W. Sockman, veteran Methodist minister in New York, said, "In our time, the church's fault is not, as some would say, that she speaks too seldom. Rather, she speaks too often and on too many subjects . . . . Churchmen act as though they feel they have to pontificate on any problem and, having spoken, tend to assume that there is little more to be said. This is boorish behavior as well as bad theology. It leaves little alternative for those who disagree but to stay away. Thoughtful members of contemporary society are doing this in droves."

One newspaper columnist commented on pulpit preoccupation with politics: "Reason, restraint, and moderation too often are overwhelmed. The cacophony mounts; and the congregations decline."

But there's another side to this, too, Some people are staying away from our churches because what goes on in church never touches down where people live, never gets into the cracks where our communities are splitting apart, never makes any timely difference. We church people can be like Rip Van Winkle, who slept through a revolution. But some persons have neither the talent nor the time for that sort of spiritual irresponsibility. So they go somewhere else where they think the action really is.

Now if we refuse to go so far as to reject religion entirely or even to reject the form of religion, what is left? What can we do if we are dissatisfied with religion as usual, religion weighted down with an intolerable load of self-preoccupation?

I believe the answer is suggested in the words of the text: Let the form of religion be infused with reality, with vitality. Give religion free rein. Let the knowledge of God cover the earth as the waters cover the sea. Let this faith in God and this devotion to him take form and captivate our imagination, engage our senses, and conquer our will.

IV

But let's not permit our enthusiasm to run away with us. The matter is not easily resolved.

For one thing, the form and the quality of religion may not be compatible. They may be like what English essayist Sydney Smith described—like triangular bits of wood in square holes, oblong in triangular, square in round. Let's look at the Free Church tradition. The form of that faith says that every man is free to interpret the Bible for himself; free to reach his own conclusions as he lets the Holy Spirit guide him. A coerced faith is no faith at all. Yet some who give lip service to freedom deny with their deeds what their lips are saying. They call people heretics who disagree with them, mount misleading campaigns against them, and seek to ban their books. The trouble is that they preserve the outward form of freedom, make pronouncements on it, pass resolutions for it, but their works and their influence are a standing denial of honest belief in it.

On the other hand, a different tradition may openly deny the right of an individual to be wrong. It may use its own power or the power of government to control public expressions of independent religious opinion. This had been done, and persons like John Bunyan, Roger Williams, and Teilhard de Chardin have had heavy, unnecessary burdens laid upon them. In this case, the form of religion, intolerant bigotry, is bad, for it will not accommodate the burgeoning good within it, to say nothing of what is good outside it.

Jesus said, "No one sews a patch of unshrunk cloth to an old coat, for then the patch tears away from the coat, and leaves a bigger hole. Neither do you put new wine into old wine-skins; if you do, the skins burst, and then the wine runs out and the skins are spoilt. No, you put new wine into fresh skins; then both are preserved" (Matt. 9:16–17, NEB).

Our Lord said these words to justify his unorthodox approach to human need. Jesus came to do the will of God, and if the Temple stood in the way of God's will, then the Temple had to go; if a long-revered custom stood in the way, it had to go; if a stubborn, close-minded individual stood in the way, he had to change or be left behind.

Suppose Jesus had had to get official approval from the established religion of his time? How far, do you think, would he have got? To begin with, some people had certain suspicions about his parentage. Others tried to suppress his teaching, for many of his views differed from their own. If the officials had approved him, they would have swallowed him up with flattery or committee meetings, and either can be lethal.

Jesus' religion was new wine, and it had to have new wineskins to contain it, skins flexible and resilient enough to expand with its new life and not break, durable enough to last in time of testing.

And that is what people in growing numbers are thinking about the church. The church as it is represented in some places is like an old wineskin; brittle, unresilient, unaccommodative to new, vital pressures within. So what happens to it? In some cases, the wineskin, the church, bursts dramatically, and the wine, the new life, is dissipated and lost in the explosion. In other cases, the wineskin, the church, springs a leak, and the wine, the new life, is lost gradually, almost unnoticed, while the old wineskin hangs intact, admired for sentimental reasons that have to do more with antiquity than with relevance.

There's nothing wrong with institutions per se. But there's plenty wrong with a fixed institutionalism that resists growth and change, that slays its prophets, and that denies its service to the modern world.

We love our institutions—home, school, nation, church. We sing of them: "Be it ever so humble, there's no place like home"; "Hail to thee, dear Alma Mater"; "My country, 'tis of thee."

> I love thy church, O God!
> Her walls before thee stand,
> Dear as the apple of thine eye,
> And graven on thy hand.

And we should love all of them; home, school, nation, church. But we must not kill them or bury them alive by not helping them to reproduce their vitality and discover their adaptability.

The Chinese used to cripple their little girls for life by binding their feet in the name of beauty. Christians may cripple the church by wrapping it unwittingly in the grave clothes of an outlived tradition and placing it tenderly in a tomb of irrelevance in the name of authority and security. New life and fitting forms is what the times call for. And that may make astonishing demands upon all of us! It may not mean that our cherished institutions will be swept away. When Christianity burst upon the first-century world, the Temple of awesome beauty and haunting tradition went with the wind, but the synagogue, simple, functional remained, though transformed in the shape of the earliest Christian churches. So all was not lost; the best was preserved. Religious life went on, though vastly changed.

V

Well, what do you think about it? What I have been saying is, I believe, not merely a private opinion, but a judgment of history.

To reject vital religion will require nothing of us. Just let life, even religious life, go on as usual, and it will cease to be a vital force in you. You may argue for it; you may fight for it; you may even die for it; and yet it may hold no more value for you than allegiance to a political faction, to a family tradition, or to a mental quirk.

The apostle Paul could see that outward declarations of piety don't always jibe with what a man really is. He said, "Men will love nothing but money and self; they will be arrogant, boastful, and abusive; with no respect of parents, no gratitude, no piety, no natural affection; they will be implacable in their hatreds, scandalmongers, intemperate and fierce, strangers to all goodness, traitors, adventurers, swollen with self-importance. They will be men who put pleasure in the place of God, men who preserve the outward form of religion, but are a standing denial of its reality" (2 Tim. 3:2–5, NEB).

To reject religion as a vital force in one's life can lead to such extremes. You don't have to be all hot and angry about it. Just let yourself go, and there are no depths to which you cannot sink. And all the while you may proudly wave a flag with the words inscribed, "Faith of Our Fathers." It is a sad fact that an individual or a nation can go to hell with all the banners waving, all the trumpets blowing, and all the church bells ringing. But to quote another New Testament writer dealing with similar matters: "Although we give these words of warning we feel sure that you, whom we love, are capable of better things and will enjoy the full experience of salvation" (Heb. 6:9, Phillips).

I said that to reject vital religion will require nothing of us. However, to allow faith to come alive does require something.

We have to recapture a vision of God's will for the individual, for the church, and for the world. Not what I want, not what the church wants, not what the world wants, but what God wants is all-important; this will continually call the church to reformation; this will constantly call into being new forms of devotion and service and invest old forms with fresh vitality; this will take away some of the shame of our powerless religious institutions and give them a significance that far outweighs their present social prestige and political power.

We must remember that the symbol of the church is not the life-extending apparatus of the geriatric ward, but the cross. And the goal of the church is not self-preservation, but self-giving.

8
Why Pray?

Luke 2:25–35; Matthew 7:7, RSV

"Ask . . . Seek . . . Knock"

"The curse of so much religion," George Meredith is quoted to have said, "is that men cling to God with their weakness rather than with their strength."

Do you believe that?

As I look into my own life, I have to admit, "Yes, it is true—too true. I have often clung to God in weak resignation." I have said, "Why concern myself with this or that? God knows what he is doing." Or I have said, "I'll be satisfied with what I am and what I do. Why be rash and try to play God?"

Many things I read in the Bible disturb me. I read the words of Jesus, "Ask, and it will be given you; seek, and you will find; knock, and it will be opened to you." These words disturb me when I discover that I am to ask and keep on asking; seek and keep on seeking; knock and keep on knocking. Keep on praying? Some of us have hardly prayed about some things the first time!

The need to pray—prayer defined by the literal meaning of the English word *pray*—is a basic and continuing need of everyone. More than that, God himself needs our prayers to help him do some things that would not be done without those prayers.

But here is our temptation. We can have our devotional fervor turned on or off by the latest theologian or philosopher we have read. The need to pray, however, is persistent. We may put to sleep that need with a massive dose of hyper-Calvinism, or we may bind and gag it with a brash Stoicism, but the need stays with us.

I

We should not be surprised if an imp sits on our shoulder
and whispers, "You can't change God's mind. So why pray?"

That assertion is frighteningly close to the truth. Some of the
words of the Bible almost say that. "For ever, O Lord, thy word
is firmly fixed in the heavens," says the psalmist (119:89, RSV).
But he doesn't quite say, "You can't change God's mind." He
does tell us that Jehovah differs from the gods of the heathen,
for the Lord is predictable. He is faithful and reliable.

Or, consider what Paul has to say: "For those whom he fore-
knew he also predestined to be conformed to the image of his
Son. . . . And those whom he predestined he also called; and
those whom he called he also justified" (Rom. 8:29–30, RSV).
This tells us that God's mind is made up about one thing in
particular—the redemption of humankind. His eternal purpose
is a purpose of love and grace. When Jesus came, he underscored
that fact. Who would want it different? We are resigned to that.
No, more than being merely resigned to it, we can welcome it,
embrace it, affirm it with our whole being.

On the other hand, there is that aspect of the will of God
which is not welcomed, not embraced, not affirmed. When God
visits us with suffering, sorrow, and death, we indeed "wince"
and "cry aloud." Will meets will. Our mind struggles with the
mind of God. There is a modern reenactment of the ancient drama
of Jacob wrestling with the angel, the Ninevites repenting so
that God will repent, or Jesus saying in anguish, "Father, if it
be possible, let this cup pass from me" (Matt. 26:39).

The audacity of it is breathtaking. Do I, a mortal man, dare
put on my shoes and stand up to God? The deed is done when
I don't like what is happening to me or to someone else and
register my complaint with God, or even when I am bold enough

to confront God with the restless yearnings of my heart. Am I being blasphemous or insolent to pray in that manner?

If so, then Epictetus, the Stoic, sounded better than many Christians when he prayed, "Give me what Thou desirest for me. For I know that what Thou choosest for me is far better than what I could choose." Brother Lawrence, who practiced the presence of God, would practically agree with Epictetus, for he said that he regarded the hours spent in the kitchen as valuable as those spent in prayer.

Some philosophers and some saints would make prayer a matter of submission only. Why fight, they seem to say, for the last chapter of this story is already written, and we know how it will come out.

P. T. Forsyth saw it differently. He said, "We need not begin with 'Thy will be done' if we but end with it."

Does God really want us to confess our impatience, to ask him questions, and to beat a path of protest to his throne of grace? It should not surprise us if he does. We are not better than our Lord. What more vivid example have we of wrestling in prayer than the picture of a solitary figure, the Son of God, praying through the night hours?

The Bible and our Lord in particular plainly teach that prayer is petition, asking, though it may have other meanings too. It seems clear also that some things simply would not happen apart from our prayers. Theologian Emil Brunner declared, "God awaits our prayer, and because He longs to extend His Kingdom not only over men but through men and with men, God accomplishes some things only when they are asked for; God earnestly awaits our prayer. We dare believe that our prayers make possible for us some action of God not otherwise possible." [1]

Can we say that God is any the less concerned with the asking than with the receiving? Is he less concerned with the seeking

than with the finding? Is he less concerned with the knocking
than with the open door? No, "He is the hunger, as well as the
food." It is as much Christian to pray *boldly* as it is to yield *graciously*.

II

Now, quite naturally we are interested in what happens as
the result of our prayers. We are practical enough for that! What
does happen?

If you pray, something will happen to you. The one who prays
finds a hand to guide him when the way is dark. He discovers
he can go on in spite of failure, sickness, and even sin. He hears
God say, "Thy sins be forgiven thee" (Matt. 9:5) and "I will
never leave thee, nor forsake thee" (Heb. 13:5). We need that!
Without seeking and finding the help of God one might wander
a lifetime in the dark, or fold up in defeat every time a strong,
opposing wind should blow, or despair of ever being at peace
with God.

These are perhaps our most urgent needs, these crises of the
spirit, but they are not our only needs that God meets through
prayer. Some of you may know that as a recent and dramatic
experience. Some of you students are at the seminary today because you prayed for your daily bread and prayed earnestly. The
answer came. And you are here.

A number of years ago, Dr. H. H. Rowley told in this chapel
a moving story of God's provision through prayer.

In response to an appeal for more liberal support of foreign
missions, an elderly lady who lived in an almshouse placed in
Dr. Rowley's hand an envelope with an extra gift of seven shill-
ings, six pence for foreign missions. Dr. Rowley, her pastor, knew
that she could not afford such an amount from her meager allow-
ance, since she had already given generously to missions. He
begged her to take it back, arguing that as the Lord was pleased
with Abraham's willingness to sacrifice Isaac, but did not require

it after all, so the Lord would be pleased with her willingness without her gift. With quiet dignity she refused, saying that she was not giving the money to her pastor.

A few days later a wealthy lady sent Dr. Rowley a check for five pounds for a service he had done her. She requested that the money be used for his work as he pleased. He went to see the lady in the almshouse. As he was leaving, he asked if she would do him the service of allowing him to leave with her a small gift, telling her of its source.

Immediately she burst into tears and told him that at the moment when he had knocked at her door she was on her knees, praying that God would somehow send her something to meet her need. She had no food and would receive no more money for three days.[2]

Does this boggle your mind? Perhaps this sort of thing astounds us too much. After all, Jesus said, "You did not choose me, but I chose you and appointed you that you should go and bear fruit and that your fruit should abide; so that whatever you ask the Father in my name, he may give it to you" (John 15:16, RSV). What might appear to be a selfish prayer may be nothing of the kind. It may really be God's indirect way of doing a significant work for his kingdom.

Prayer does cause remarkable things to happen in the life of one who prays. It can also lead to happy consequences in the lives of those one prays for. Pray for a man, and you will come to love him, care what happens to him, and, if possible, do something concrete to help him. But that is not the limit of such prayer. God uses our prayers to help those for whom we pray, even though they do not know we have prayed for them, even though we may have no contact with them except through prayer.

One of my seminary professors spoke in a class of the effect of intercessory prayer. He said that God had given him a special ministry of praying for some people whom others had given up praying for and that he had seen some of them become converted. There are many people whose lives are different because someone prayed for them, the doctrine of free will notwithstanding.

What shall we say of the prayers of those whose concern moves beyond the needs of the individuals they know? Some are distressed by the sins of mankind, by our universal fallen state, by the pain and anxiety that a world subjected to futility inflicts on its inhabitants. Are these who mourn in this way truly blessed, as Jesus said they were? Do their lifelong prayers make sense? Will their faith that rebels at last move the mountains of sin, suffering, and death?

Let us turn back the scroll of the centuries. A man of Israel bows to the ground in an agony of prayer. This man had not meekly acquiesced in the humiliation of his people before the world. He had not accepted the perdition of the heathen as a final judgment of God. He found no meaning and redemption in trying to be a well-adjusted personality in the kind of world he lived in. His prayer for a Messiah who would change what is mean and spiritually distasteful became the passion of his life. And God gave the man a hope in his striving. God revealed to him that in his lifetime he would see the Christ. Years pass. Jesus is born. Inspired by the Spirit, this man Simeon came to the Temple, where the infant Jesus was being presented to the Lord. He took the child in frail arms that now felt new strength. Tears of joy filled the sad, ascetic eyes as he blessed God and said: "Lord, now lettest thou thy servant depart in peace,/according to thy word;/for mine eyes have seen thy salvation/which thou hast prepared in the presence of all peoples,/a light for revelation to the Gentiles,/and for glory to thy people Israel" (Luke 2:29–32, RSV).

This man's prayers poured into the stream of God's purpose, as did the prayers of many others, and surely helped to bring to pass what God had willed. The Redeemer came. At last, he came! What a glorious fulfillment! But there is more.

The last prayer has not been prayed, and the last battle has not been fought. The martyrs pray, "How long, O Lord." Many other devout hearts pray, "Thy kingdom come, thy will be done in earth as it is in heaven." Some pray in the words of the Seer, "Come, Lord Jesus." And with the whole creation "groaning in travail," "nature, also, mourns for a lost good."

I have often wondered how one could be properly concerned about God's will for the present life and at the same time pray for the hastening of the Lord's return. I knew a pastor who periodically preached and prayed publicly for the second coming of Christ. His concern about it always seemed to coincide with a new crisis in his personal difficulties. He seemed to value the Parousia as a kind of deus ex machina to extract him from the messes he repeatedly got himself into.

Who will be the persons who "have loved and longed for his appearance"? I think it will be those who are so concerned about the ultimate triumph of God's purpose that they throw themselves, their strength, and their prayers into the burning challenges of the hour, with the intrepid expectation that what is but half-finished today will be completely fulfilled in God's great tomorrow.

Why pray? The magnitude of the need of my own life, the incompleteness of the lives of those I love and know, and the burden of the world's sin and suffering leave me with no alternative but to pray—if I care and God cares. God wants my prayers, asks for them, inspires them, and, amazing though it may seem, will, through those prayers, find his hand strengthened to accomplish his purpose of grace.

Simeon of old fulfilled his stewardship of prayer. Our stewardship is yet unfulfilled. So we and others must pray "until he has put all his enemies under his feet" (1 Cor. 15:25, RSV).

[1] Emil Brunner, *Our Faith* (London: SCM Press, Ltd., 1949), p. 95.
[2] H. H. Rowley, *The Relevance of the Bible* (New York: The Macmillan Co., 1948), pp. 117–18.

9

Ride On . . . to Live!

John 12:12–19

"Your King Is Coming"

Everyone of us takes some kind of attitude toward Jesus Christ. We cannot escape his presence. He is on our hands today to be received or to be rejected. And between these two poles of receiving him and rejecting him there are ways of reacting and responding to him that are partly good and partly bad.

On this very day Jesus Christ has been coming to us again. On this Palm Sunday, we anticipate Good Friday and its cross. So it is easy for us to draw a mental picture of Jesus coming to us in his humility. We can visualize him with his face turned steadfastly toward Jerusalem and his crucifixion. But his coming to us is much more than this. It is more than a vividly imagined event, more than a warm sentiment that dissolves us into ecstasy. His presence is real. He comes to us with the same work to be done, with the same life to live, and with the same death to die. But that is not all. Today he confronts again in us the same attitudes as those held by his friends and his enemies in the days of his flesh.

And now we look at Palm Sunday through the eyes of the writer of the Fourth Gospel.

During the closing days of his earthly ministry Jesus' raising of Lazarus caused great excitement among many people. Some were overjoyed. Mary and Martha, the sisters of Lazarus, could not find enough words and time to thank Jesus for what he had done for them. And there were others who went into Jerusalem and spread abroad the story of the most wonderful event they had ever witnessed. But all were not happy. John tells us that Jesus' enemies determined to kill him when he raised Lazarus from the dead. Besides that, these men planned to put Lazarus to death also.

With events shaping up for a showdown, Jesus entered Jerusalem, riding an ass's colt, and the crowds went wild. The fickle majority, a convinced minority, the twelve disciples, and the Pharisees constituted the groups involved with Jesus on Palm Sunday. Two thousand years ago, you and I could easily have been in one group or another. Today we are in such groups as Jesus Christ passes through our midst again.

I

Are you in the group that opposes Christ? I hope not, and you probably are not. But we cannot rule out the possibility that even if we imagine that we would never "hurt a hair of him," might oppose him.

When Jesus was here in the flesh, opposition to him was direct. "Now the chief priests and the Pharisees had given orders that if anyone knew where he was, he should let them know, so that they might arrest him" (John 11:57, RSV). After Palm Sunday, with all its tumult and shouting, some of the Pharisees despaired of doing anything with Jesus. They said to one another, "You see that you can do nothing; look, the world has gone after him" (John 12:19, RSV). Yet, the enemies of Jesus did not give up: "So the band of soldiers and their captain and the officers of the Jews seized Jesus and bound him" (John 18:12, RSV).

Opposition to Jesus Christ today is more subtle and sophisticated. He is not here among us physically, so we cannot crucify him again. But why did anyone oppose him in the first place? Were the reasons then any different essentially from the reasons that explain our stance toward many of the issues of our own day? Was not Jesus opposed because he threatened existing struc-

tures? Were not his opponents principally those who had considerable vested interests in these structures? Did they not fear that
the revolutionary changes Jesus seemed to favor would precipitate
conflict? The opposition to Jesus was easy to explain, and credible!
Jesus' opponents said, "What are we to do? For this man performs
many signs. If we let him go on thus, every one will believe in
him, and the Romans will come and destroy both our holy place
and our nation" (John 11:48, RSV).

Now, honestly, we are no different, are we? For centuries some
Christians tried to blame the Jewish people with the crucifixion
of Jesus, calling the Jews "Christ killers." But what did this age-
old slander accomplish? It only served to blind generations of
church people to the fact that they too, Gentiles or whatnot,
were capable of crucifying Jesus Christ.

How do we oppose Jesus Christ today? We may prefer a Christianity that is tamed and domesticated by political traditions,
by denominational biases, by racial prejudices, by social stratifica-
tions, and by personal ambitions. We may not want anyone to
take religion outside the walls of the church building. So, when
the judging and redeeming message of Jesus Christ begins to make
itself felt where custom and habit are deeply entrenched, we
may find ourselves opposing him. But it is far more likely that
our opposition to him will be a simple, uncomplicated refusal
to do what the lordship of Christ and Christian love require in
concrete instances. We will reject a clear command, or we will
decide a matter by looking the other way. Perhaps we cannot
see ourselves opposing Christ by fighting a cause or movement:
we have no quixotic notions of anything so dramatic in our com-
monplace lives. Yet, deed by deed, word by word, and thought
by thought, we may stand in his path, arms akimbo, keeping
him from making our lives what they could be.

Religion is no guarantee that one will not line up against Christ.

The Pharisees were good men, praying men, men scrupulous in their financial stewardship. Yet they were opposed to Jesus. They rejected in public and private ways that judging and saving presence, and so have his opponents of whatever century.

II

You and I may not oppose Jesus Christ, but are we in the group that praises him superficially?

Certain people were excited by the news that Jesus was coming to grips with some of the vital issues of life. He had fed the hungry thousands. He had healed the sick. He had even raised the dead. The raising of Lazarus caused no end of talk about Jesus in Jerusalem. His name was on the lips of young and old alike. You can imagine one of them saying, "This is what we have been working for and waiting for all our lives—freedom from hunger and sickness and the fear of death. Jesus can answer all our human problems. Perhaps the Messiah has come." Back and forth like a shuttlecock flew the rumors, and each time they caught another person in the warp and woof of popular enthusiasm.

It is easy to be a faddist in religion as well as in other departments of life. After the second World War, a revival of religious interest and discussion swept the United States. Church attendance picked up. Money started pouring into the collection plates. Church membership increased. Sunday sermons and revival services were like dragnets; they picked up everything, both good and bad. No longer was there any question in business or society about whether it was prudent to be an active church member. To join a church was the "in" thing to do. So many people were on the religious bandwagon that they were falling off, and nobody noticed the difference.

Where I was pastor, a department superintendent in Sunday

School said, "We find ourselves almost praying that all our enroll-
ment will not be present on a given Sunday, for we would have
no place to put them all."

Could it be that some of the problems the churches face today
stem from the superficial attractiveness of church membership
to which some persons have yielded with no real concern for
the deeper meaning of it? Christ was the answer to many of
the superficial questions we were asking, but too many of us
never got around to asking the basic questions of our existence.

Where were those crowds of people who shouted hosannas
on Palm Sunday after Jesus was crucified? Perhaps some of those
who had shouted the loudest would have said, if you had inquired
of them, "Jesus? Who is he? I never heard of the man—or very
little. I know he was crucified." But this was not necessarily the
case with all or even most of them. The faddist, the superficially
enthusiastic disciple, may develop deeper reasons for his discipleship than the general opinions that move the crowd; deeper reasons than the meeting of some grossly selfish or physical need.
The biggest job facing the church today is not that of converting
the world, but that of converting us who are already in the church.
Elton Trueblood, in *The Yoke of Christ* called the church our greatest
mission field.

III

Now you and I may belong neither to the group that opposes
Jesus Christ nor to the group that is enchanted with him for a
while, only to fall aside soon or late. Are we among those who
take him seriously?

Those who witnessed Jesus' raising of Lazarus took Jesus seriously. What they saw and heard and felt, they could never forget.
It was a part of their fund of experience. Moth and rust could
not corrupt it, and the thief of time could not take it away. Every
thought about God and about life would, from that time forward,

have to be with reference to what Jesus did at Bethany. Those witnesses were the persons who spread the report in Jerusalem of what Jesus had done. But all of this did not mean that the witnesses were necessarily converted by what they had seen, heard, and felt.

We too may be profoundly impressed with the evidence for the Christian faith. There is much evidence, and much of it is convincing. The miracles of Jesus, his resurrection and appearances after his resurrection, the outpouring of the Spirit on the day of Pentecost, the courage and fidelity of the disciples, and the tremendous effectiveness of the early church have through the centuries carried remarkable apologetic weight. They have helped millions believe the truth of the Christian faith. Yet there are many persons in the twentieth century who delude themselves with the notion that if they can accumulate enough convincing facts to overwhelm their intellect they will become Christian believers. Could it be that some of us imagine ourselves to be true Christians just because we do not have any religious questions or doubts? We have accepted a certain set of facts and subscribed to a certain set of doctrines. We know the Bible well and can argue glibly about it. We may even be theological students or theological professors. (And I do not have to tell you, there are definite advantages to having a sound religious upbringing!) But is there nothing more to faith than knowing a great number of important facts and assenting to a system of beautiful beliefs?

Do you take Jesus Christ seriously? Can you read and discuss the Bible intelligently? Does your ethical life correspond to your beliefs? If so, then you may not be far from the kingdom of God. You may be in it. There are many such people in the kingdom of God. To them, the Christian faith is a reasonable way of believing. To them, the Christian life is a responsible way of living. They accept the faith and live the life. It is as simple as that. On the other hand, there are those who are ever learning, as the apostle Paul put it, ever learning but never able to come to the knowledge of the truth. They would agree with almost anything reasonable that you might say about the Christian faith and perhaps insist that they would not want to live in a community or a country that did not have such faith. But for them the Christian faith remains a matter for discussion and a question yet to be settled.

IV

So, we may oppose Jesus; we may lightly praise him; or we may be everlastingly haunted by his reality, but never quite committed to him. On the other hand, could we be among those who are truly his friends, truly sharing his cross?

The Danish philosopher, Kierkegaard, brought the matter into focus when he prayed, "O Lord Jesus Christ, thou didst not come into the world for the sake of being ministered to, nor surely to be worshipped in the sense of being admired. Thou thyself wast the way and the truth. Thou didst demand followers, not admirers. So, wake us up if we have dozed off into delusion; save us from going astray by wishing merely to admire thee, when the thing that is needful is to want to follow thee, and be made like unto thee."

The disciples of Jesus, excepting Judas Iscariot, were willing to go with him to the death. It is strange, is it not, that no matter how many wandering stars blazed and flickered and disappeared about Jesus, those disciples kept their courses around him, like planets around a central sun, in spite of cloud and storm and darkness? But should it be strange and incredible?

The Christian faith is certainly not something to be opposed. And just as surely, it is not something merely to rave about with hollow praise or with which to play intellectual games. The Christian faith is to be lived and died for. We sing in our Palm Sunday hymn, "Ride on to die!" Where did this idea come from, if not from Jesus himself? He said, "Truly, truly, I say to you, unless a grain of wheat falls into the earth and dies, it remains alone; but if it dies, it bears much fruit" (John 12:24, RSV). In the Synoptic Gospels, Jesus says in one form or other, "Take up your cross and follow me"—and a cross means death!

Now if Christian discipleship meant death and nothing more, it would be a form of suicide and totally reprehensible. And unfortunately that is all that some persons see in it: the death of happiness, the death of friendship, the death of human striving, the death of freedom. But Jesus referred to his crucifixion as his glorification. As Eduard Schweizer puts it in *God's Inescapable Nearness* (tr. by James W. Cox, Word Books, 1971), "Just as the grain of wheat must die, must decompose, in order that the full ear of grains of wheat might come from it, so must the one Jesus die. He must die in order not to remain for himself alone but that a community might be born which really belongs with him, a community for which he remains not merely an image that a man gazes at, admiringly, but the one with whom a man can live and die." To die with Jesus really means to give up self. This may not be required all at once. It seldom is. We may have to die daily, giving a bit of self here, a bit there, until it all adds up to what can only be called "taking up his cross" or offering ourself as "a living sacrifice." Luther saw the full scope of the demand when he penned the words of "A Mighty Fortress Is Our God."

> Let goods and kindred go,
> This mortal life also;
> The body they may kill:
> God's truth abideth still,
>   His Kingdom is forever.

You and I can take our stand this side of the resurrection of our Lord and see that the call to death is actually a summons to life. Crucifixion is actually glorification. Our meager self-denials and sufferings are gaining for us a richness of life out of all proportion to what we give up. So the words of the hymn, "Ride on to die!" really mean, "Ride on to live!" for the cross of humiliation has opened the door to the triumph of the resurrection. And to those of us who walk with him he says, "Because I live, you will live also" (John 14:19, RSV).

10
Faith and the Resurrection

1 Corinthians 15:1–28

"In Christ Shall All Be Made Alive"

What is Easter all about? It is a joyous time. Spring is bursting out all over. The gray days of winter are gone except for an occasional reminder. All nature leaps to the challenge to create.

What is Easter all about? It is a happy coincidence of the resourcefulness of earth and the resoucefulness of heaven. But it is especially about God and what he did about a tragic event of two thousand years ago, and it is about what he continues to do in face of the tragedies of your personal history and mine. In a word, Easter is about the resurrection of Jesus Christ and what that means to you and to me.

Easter came as a surprise to the early disciples. They were not expecting it, but it happened anyway. And they could never get through talking about it. Because they believed it and went everywhere talking about it, telling the good news that their crucified Lord had arisen from the dead, the church sprang to life like some young giant born full grown. They did not give us a clear picture of how it all happened—what God did when he raised Jesus from the dead—but they left no room to doubt that it did happen, gloriously, victoriously.

I cannot explain the resurrection. Yet, I can believe it; I can experience its power; I can affirm and proclaim it. And so I do, with a thankful, hopeful, and joyful heart. I pray that God will make this a festival of renewal of faith by giving us eyes to see and hearts to believe the remarkable consequences of our Lord's resurrection.

I

In the first place, because God raised Jesus Christ from the dead, we can believe that our sins are forgiven. I am taking it for granted that you and I still believe in the reality of sin—those things that we have done which we ought not to have done, and those things that we have left undone which we ought to have done. I speak of whatever it is that separates you from God, that makes you feel at a distance from him and estranged from him, or that makes you feel guilty. You may not think about it all the time, but whenever you think about it you know it is true. You know it especially and painfully when you have failed.

I suppose that no personality in the Bible presents our situation so well as Simon Peter. In our human weaknesses and failures, all of us can identify with him. We are so much like him. We love God and are committed to Jesus Christ; we have good intentions; we want to serve our Lord, and we promise to serve him. In some euphoric moments, we even fancy we would die for him. But like Simon Peter, we get under pressure. Nothing is so real at the moment as the pressure. God, right, good intentions, vows, and conscience can hardly be heard. Only the steady, dinning torture of physical desire, of the need for social approval, of the demand for money or power gets through to us. And then what happens? We yield to the pressure; we sin; we deny our Lord. After we have realized what we have done, too late to reverse our decision, we are demoralized. We know that we have wronged our Lord. We can scarcely believe that we belong to him. Like Simon Peter, we may go out and weep bitterly.

But it is when we have sinned that he comes to us. Actually, he has been present all along, though we have not recognized his presence. But how obvious his presence when we have sinned!

In that moment, we want both to run from him and to cry out to him. And he comes to us for that's his business, for he is the Savior.

He says, "You have done wrong. You know it. No one has to tell you. And now you are saying to yourself, 'I really never knew him.' But you do belong to me. I knew what you were when I called you to follow me. I also knew what you could become. You have failed me, but you still belong to me. You will bear my name forever. You may deny me a thousand times, but because you belong to me, I will make you confess me a thousand times. I have carried the burden of your sin, and I will carry it again."

What pain such words of love can inflict! Like a father's look of disappointment or like a mother's tears, our Lord's persistent commitment to us makes us see what sin is and what it does. It makes us see that our cowardly silence and our indolent neglect, as well as our feverish acts of disobedience, are betrayal and crucifixion of him, new denials and new wounds compounded of the same evils that did him to death two thousand years ago. And so comes the haunting question:

> Once, oh, once I crucified him.
> Shall I crucify my Lord again?

But that is not all. He does not come to avenge the wrongs we have done him. He comes not to avenge, but to save. He forgives us freely and fully, saying, "Go, and sin no more," knowing full well that we will sin again and again. And still he is willing to take upon himself once more the burden of our guilt and the humiliation of our dishonor. For where sin abounds, grace abounds much more. He is determined that love shall at last win the victory over all our sins.

II

Not only can we believe that our sins are forgiven because God raised Jesus Christ from the dead, we can believe also in a future life in Christ.

Those who walk with Jesus Christ, who enter into the struggles and triumphs of fellowship with him, realize that this new life and relationship is the beginning of something that has no end. The apostle Paul said, "Therefore, if any one is in Christ, he is a new creation; the old has passed away, behold, the new has come" (2 Cor. 5:17, RSV). Because of Christ, life has a new quality, a new dimension. The Fourth Gospel calls it "eternal life." It is something of the life of God himself brought into our existence. That is why we hear Jesus say, "And this is life eternal, that they might know thee the only true God, and Jesus Christ, whom thou hast sent" (John 17:3). And that is why the apostle Paul said, "For to me to live is Christ, and to die is gain" (Phil. 1:21). As Paul saw it, "To depart and be with Christ . . . is far better" (Phil. 1:23).

Now let me ask: How could Paul have felt this way if Christ has not been raised? How could you and I have radiant certitude and hope about the future if Christ has not been raised? Our belief about the future life is based on the risen Christ. It is inextricably tied up with him. He is the firstfruits, the first harvest, of those who have died. And he says to us as we shudder at the thought of our own death, "Because I live, you shall live also" (John 14:19).

Perhaps you have asked yourself dozens of times, "What will the next world be like?" And it is only natural that you should. On Easter 1965 I preached in New York City. In my sermon I said, "Next Thursday I am scheduled to sail for Europe for my first visit. I have wondered over and over again what it will be like. I've read books, I've talked to people, I've used my imagination, and I've tried to prepare for the new experiences I will have. But I am sure there will be many surprises. As to heaven, I am convinced that none of the speculations of men, even the fabulous visions of apostles, prophets, and seers can do justice to what awaits us there. If we have walked with the living Christ, surely we have some idea of what it is like." My subsequent sojourn in Europe, with its gratifying fulfillment and happy surprises, persuaded me that my analogy was reasonable and proper.

We can be certain of this: God will handle your death and mine in a way best suited to his purposes and to our needs. I do not quarrel with my Creator about this life that he has given me, nor do I question his wisdom and love with respect to the next world. I was born into a world compatible with my physical needs; I received a Savior adequate to my spiritual needs. Surely I can trust God to meet whatever the next world requires.

But did it ever puzzle you that the Bible speaks a great deal about resurrection and very little about immortality? And when it speaks about immortality, it is either a quality that God alone possesses or it is something that we "put on," not something that we possess by nature. "For this perishable nature must put on the imperishable, and this mortal nature must put on immortality" (1 Cor. 15:53, RSV). The robust way in which the Bible speaks should comfort us. For the Bible talks in terms of the reconstitution of the redeemed personality. We shall be total persons, not just disembodied spirits floating aimlessly in space. So the term resurrection, rather than immortality, is the biblical term, the rich word that describes the future life of those who belong to Jesus Christ. And as Paul makes plain, our resurrection will not be a gathering together of our individual dust and ashes, but a giving to each of us as individuals "a body as he has chosen" (1 Cor. 15:38, RSV). That is, as it has pleased God. "Beloved," wrote John, "we are God's children now; it does not yet appear what we shall be, but we know that when he appears we shall be like him, for we shall see him as he is" (1 John 3:2, RSV).

III

Now all of this is wonderfully comforting to believe, but it is not enough. One other conviction must complete the triad. Because God raised Jesus Christ from the dead, we can believe in the ultimate victory of God. The resurrection of Christ is the decisive clue to the meaning of the universe and the final purpose of God. The truth of the resurrection is of cosmic proportions.

The purpose of God to redeem includes not only the forgiveness of sins and the life everlasting. All creation shares in his redemption. Borrowing a figure from the process of natural birth, Paul described the whole creation as groaning and travailing in pain together, awaiting God's final act of redemption. The God revealed in Jesus Christ, who brought him again from the dead, this God is infinitely resourceful and redemptive. Nothing can stop him from achieving his purpose. Sin is an obstacle—he conquered it in the cross. Death is an obstacle—he conquered it in the resurrection. All the evil in an untamed universe is an obstacle—he will conquer it when, to use the words of the apostle Peter, we see "new heavens and a new earth in which righteousness dwells" (2 Pet. 3:13, RSV).

Again and again, the momentary victories of evil—crime, sickness, death, floods, and tornadoes—confront us with the cross and its tragedy. These victories of evil seem to be saying to us, "God is dead." And circumstances sometimes force us to live out many of our days in the noonday darkness of Good Friday. But Easter says to us, "God is alive. God has won the victory over sin and death. The power of the enemy is broken." It was this assurance that rescued the disciples from defeat, discouragement, and despair and made them the heralds of the good news to the ends of the earth. It is this assurance that can defeat the power of sin over us, that can give us something eternal to hope for, and that can make us bow ever more humbly before the loving Father who will make all things new and who will be "all in all."

11
Help for the Downhearted

Psalm 42

"My Soul Thirsts for God"

The forty-second Psalm pictures for us a man who has been wrenched out of his home setting and taken away as an exile. Imagination takes us back to that day when this man of pride and position was led away as an animal would be led away. Strong men wept openly for him. Others looked on in stunned curiosity. He said a hurried good-bye, and his captors took him away. Crushed, humiliated, uncertain about his future, he stumbled along in his private darkness. I can imagine that just before Jerusalem vanished behind him, he turned and took one last look at the Temple, the ancient meeting place of God and man, and his frame trembled with a stifled sob. But this was only the beginning of sorrows. Later, when his humiliation had settled down to the daily routine of waiting and despairing and waiting and despairing all over again, he cried: "As the hart panteth after the water brooks, so panteth my soul after thee, O God. My soul thirsteth for God, for the living God: when shall I come and appear before God?" (Ps. 42:1–2). Life for him as he now must live it, seemed meaningless.

Some of us know at least a measure of what this man must have felt. We have felt it, too. We know what it is to be lonely, cut off from familiar comforts, cut off from former friends, cut off from satisfying work. Some honest thinkers have known this as ostracism. Some good people who have made moral mistakes they have long ago repented of and given up have known this as a wall of separation from their neighbors. Some ill and handicapped persons have felt this as solitary confinement. You may be surrounded by thousands of people and yet feel completely alone and frustrated. If God seems far away, the pain is even sharper.

What help is there for us when we feel this way? Perhaps the psalmist can point us toward help and his experience of spiritual poverty can enrich us.

I

We can say at once that it does not help to believe that trouble doesn't happen to religious people. Yet, we are constantly haunted by self-doubt, which often turns into doubt of God. When trouble comes to us, when God seems far away, we may ask, "What have I done? What sin have I committed?" Then, when relief does not come soon, we may protest, "What kind of God would let this happen to me? Could a God of love let me be so terribly unhappy?"

But to insist that God must exempt us from trouble, to insist that God must heap health and happiness upon Christians and let the rest of the world take the scraps is a dead-end street, which leads us to a blank wall. Life has plainly written for us all to read: Sometimes good people suffer and sometimes bad people prosper; sometimes we are responsible for our troubles and successes and sometimes we are not.

II

We can also say that it does not help to believe that because you are separated from relatives and from familiar ways of worship you are separated from God.

The psalmist couldn't imagine that there was much of God to know away from Jerusalem. How easy it would be for some of us to agree with him. The hometown and the home church have a peculiar magic for us. God may have seemed more real to us there than anywhere else. We remember, perhaps with homesickness, our father's advice, our mother's prayers, our baptism, our fellow church member's encouragement, the old hymns, and the romance and idealism of youth. Could God ever again be so near or so real?

But if men had always let such sentiments guide them, our many wonderful churches would not be here. In fact, the gospel would never have gotten outside Jerusalem.

III

Furthermore, we can say that it does not help to believe that your enemies may be right or victorious simply because they are strong. The psalmist's captors hurled at him the question, "Where is thy God?" Though it cut him to the heart to hear it, he was inclined to echo the same question in his own secret thoughts. Pavlov did not invent "brainwashing." The psalmist's enemies were about to undermine his faith. Have you had this happen to you? It can happen almost before you know it. For example, you may have faithfully practiced your religious faith for years. And you have found help in the company of your friends who believe as you believe. But now you have met other people of some stature and influence, and they don't believe what you believe, perhaps even smile at it. So what has happened to you? Are you beginning to doubt that you were right in the first place? Take another example. Suppose you have made a serious mistake sometime in the past. God has forgiven you, yet some people have never forgiven you. And what does that do to you? Their superior attitude and their opinion of you tempts you to accept their judgment, though God has pronounced you forgiven.

IV

So when things have gone wrong for us, it doesn't help to believe that trouble doesn't happen to God's people. It doesn't help to believe that because you are separated from home and from familiar ways of worship you are separated from God. It doesn't help to believe that your enemies may be right or victorious just because they are strong. But it does help to wait upon God, to hope in God. The psalmist kept on saying to himself, "Why art thou cast down, O my soul? and why art thou disquieted in me? hope thou in God." If we say to ourselves in times of trouble and difficulty, "Hope in God, wait upon him," then we may later discover that God himself was speaking to us through these very words.

Isn't it true that God has promised to help us? The ancient Jews saw this as a covenant or contract. They believed that the God who created the heavens and the earth had somehow entered into their history, that on his own initiative he had made certain promises to Abraham, Isaac, and Jacob, and that he had shown himself for them by delivering the nation from slavery in Egypt, with great signs and wonders. So there was every reason to hope in God, to wait for him. He had promised to be their God and to help them. And isn't the promise yours and mine too? Don't we have also, besides all that this man knew, the fact of Jesus Christ and all the truth that surrounds him to make us sure that God will never forget us? In many wonderful ways, God has said to us, "I will never leave thee, nor forsake thee" (Heb. 13:5).

God may help us in totally unexpected ways. The psalmist, of course, could think of God's help chiefly in God's making it possible for him to go back to Jerusalem and to the Temple, with everything just as it was before he was exiled. If God— rather I should say *when* God brought him back to the Temple, then he would praise God, then he would "confess" God as his salvation. We have no way of knowing how matters finally worked out for the psalmist. Perhaps he got exactly what he longed for and expected. But you and I know that God often takes care of our problems in new and creative ways. Professor Herbert Farmer once said, "In the solitary places of human hearts is to be found the meeting place of God and man." And yonder was the psalmist imagining that this meeting place was only in a certain city, in a certain Temple. The solitary experience may be on a bed of sickness as it was for Hezekiah. It may be in the midst of persecution as it was for Jeremiah. It may be within a nation in exile as it was for Ezekiel. It may be on a cross as it was for Jesus. But in every case, God was there—and never more truly than when our Lord was crucified outside the city wall. Where is your solitary place?

Once the poet William Cowper stood at the threshold of one of the most important hours of his life, dreadfully afraid he would fail. He drove out into the country determined to kill himself. But as he was about to carry out his decision, a sudden and terrifying thunderstorm came up and so frightened Cowper that he got back into his carriage and went home. Out of that experience he wrote the words of "God Moves in a Mysterious Way."

> God moves in a mysterious way, His wonders to perform;
> He plants his footsteps in the sea And rides upon the storm.
> Ye fearful saints, fresh courage take: The clouds ye so much dread
> Are big with mercy, and shall break In blessings on your head.

What does this mean but that regardless of the way God finally works out the pattern of our lives we can still praise him? Kagawa, the Japanese Christian leader, cried, "I am God's gambler. For him I have wagered my last mite." And he put it well, for none of us knows how matters will work out for us. Yet we can keep on believing in God. God is a great mystery and always will be. But he is an abyss of love, a love we can trust though never fully understand. We can say with the psalmist, "I shall again praise him, my help and my God" (v. 11, RSV). You and I can dare praise him now.

12
Hope Unashamed

Romans 5:1–5

"Hope Does Not Disappoint Us"

Every few years a different religious idea pops up, and it would seem that we almost wear it out talking about it. The idea of hope is one of the latest of those ideas. Just now we are discussing theologies of hope; and it is plural, for there are different kinds of futures which one may hope for. However, even though we are talking about hope much more than we did just a few years ago, this truth has had a durable life; it has never worn out. Hope, as an essential ingredient of the Christian faith, has never completely dropped out of our vocabulary, though it has been sometimes ignored.

In the magnificent thirteenth chapter of 1 Corinthians, the apostle Paul mentions hope, along with faith and love, as one of the abiding realities: "So faith, hope, love abide, these three; but the greatest of these is love" (1 Cor. 13:13, RSV). The symbol that has long stood before the United States Naval Academy chapel, in Annapolis, is an anchor which also bears the form of a cross. This anchor with the cross is the abiding symbol of hope.

Do we need hope in these days? Since we talk so much about it, it must be especially necessary. We need hope because of our everyday discouragements and vexations and frustrations. When life becomes cluttered, hope offers a way through. Also, occasional crises arise, such as illness, persecution, failure, marital difficulty, and bereavement. Hope enables us to survive these seismic tremors at the foundations of our existence. But it is the inevitably of death which all of us face that offers the most sweeping chal-

lenge of all. Without hope, a pall hangs over the sweetness of
every infant, the beauty of every flower, and the grace of every
virtue. Therefore, let us examine this shining word that God has
thrust among us in the midst of darkness, defeat, and death.

I want to say three simple things. First, hope is ours. Second,
hope is hard-won. And third, hope is reliable.

I

First of all, then, the apostle tells us that hope is ours: "We
rejoice in our hope of sharing the glory of God" (Rom. 5:2, RSV).

Now there are different levels of hope. When we use the word,
we can mean different things.

One kind of hope may be only wishful thinking. Charles Dick-
ens's Mr. Macawber is a man who lives impecuniously, hoping
that his luck will improve tomorrow. In and out of debtor's prison
for nonpayment of his bills, he keeps hoping that his ship will
come in, that tomorrow will be better than today. The main problem is that he never undergirds any of his hopes with honest
toil. For him hope is a substitute for work. The American humor-
ist, Josh Billings, once said, "I never knew a man who lived on
hope but what spent his old age at somebody else's expense."
If the world's leaders keep hoping that problems created by the
population explosion in certain parts of the world will go away
and yet do nothing significant about it, then we are headed for
disaster. If we continue to pollute the air and water, hoping that
everything will be all right, and do nothing significant to correct
the problem, then, again, we are headed for disaster. If we continue to waste our natural resources as if they were inexhaustible,
hoping that there will always be enough to meet our human
needs, then, once again, disaster awaits us.

Another kind of hope is reasonable expectation. A man is in-
jured in an automobile accident. The family is filled with anxiety
about his recovery. He receives the best medical attention, and

after a consultation among the doctors, one of them says to the family, "You have every reason to hope for the best." Their experience with similar cases makes it possible for them to offer hope, for there is reasonable expectation of recovery.

However, the hope the apostle speaks of is certainly more than wishful thinking, more even than reasonable expectation: it is confident assurance. Assurance of what? Assurance of sharing the glory of God. That is, through our faith in Jesus Christ, we have the confident assurance that we will partake in God's triumph over sin and death. When Dr. D. E. King, a well-known Negro preacher from Chicago, was asked why the Christians in the black churches have always been so joyful in their worship, even when things were going very badly for them everywhere else, he said, "We rejoice in what we are going to have." Indeed, regardless of what is happening around us, regardless of our discouragements, our crises, and the grim fact of death itself, we can rejoice—not because of our troubles, but because of what we are going to have. We can enjoy the confident assurance that we shall share the glory of God. This glorious assurance is ours for the taking.

II

Now let us go a step further. The apostle also tells us that hope is hard-won: "Suffering produces endurance, and endurance produces character and character produces hope" (Rom. 5:3–4, RSV).

Hope at its best lies at the end of a long road.

Hope at its best begins in suffering. If one suffers, hope may seem and actually be far, far away. But for Anton Boisen, hope began in a mental hospital where he was a patient. For Dostoevski, the Russian novelist, hope began as he stood before a firing squad for execution and received a last minute reprieve. For Ernest Gordon, chaplain at Princeton University, hope began in the filth, stench, and death of a Japanese concentration camp during World War II, where, as a prisoner and an agnostic, a new window on life was opened up for him. In still other kinds of suffering, hope for many persons has had its first frail beginnings. Hope followed hard on the heels of failure, of illness, and of discouragement.

On the way to hope, suffering produces endurance. When an athlete is training for the *big* game, it is suffering that produces the endurance necessary for the real performance. Sometimes he may think his lungs will burst and he will almost scream from the agony of his training, but it is this very suffering that produces the endurance necessary to win when the actual contest takes place. Suffering is bearable if it has meaning, if it looks forward to something, if it has a goal. Suffering is transformed by meaning. My maternal grandmother was an invalid for several years. She never complained, but in answer to a question, she said, "I suffer death every minute." Once she said to me, "I don't know why I have to suffer as I do, but I believe I'll understand sometime." Suffering actually produced a triumphant endurance that lasted through those years.

Endurance produces character and brings God's approval. As you endure, your value system changes. Little by little, you learn what is important in life and what is unimportant, what is worth striving for and what is empty of meaning; you learn why what God expects of you and plans for you is more important than what you had planned for yourself. In other words, what you work for and what you expect gradually come into line with what God wills for you. It is little wonder, then, that the poet Keats, wrote: "The world is the vale of soul-making." God must look at the souls of men and women who have endured all kinds of sufferings and achieved unusual depths of character and integrity, and say, as he said after he had created the world and man, "It is good . . . it is very good."

God's approval creates hope. When one is sure that God has

accepted him, that God has affirmed him, that God has said *yes* to him, he has reason to hope. "We belong to God" was Israel's conviction. In all of the nation's shifting fortunes, Israel believed that God was on her side. Even when God opposed the nation, even when God brought the nation into defeat in battle and exile, Israel never ceased to hope, to have the radiant assurance that all of this was the work of God, creating a marvelous future. Of course, the people often doubted and complained. Their prophets remonstrated with God, like Tevye, in *Fiddler on the Roof,* who asked the Lord why he couldn't choose someone else once in a while.

If you know that God is on your side, though he sometimes may punish you, you never have to give up hoping. You may even sing in the words of the Broadway musical, *South Pacific,* "I can't get it out of my heart."

III

And now a final step. The apostle tells us that hope is reliable: "And hope does not disappoint us, because God's love has been poured into our hearts through the Holy Spirit which has been given to us" (Rom. 5:5, RSV).

This hope of which the apostle speaks is reliable because it rests on God alone. True hope is not built on our intelligence, our performance, our character, or our connections. Our wisdom, our works, our goodness, and our friends at some point fall short of the glory of God. Though we are created in the image of God, our humanity is forever showing through and in one way or another dishonoring God and bringing shame to ourselves. The future into which God is leading us can never be built on the foundations of human achievement. God has to work with sin and failure and defeat and death. It was William Manson who said, "The only God the New Testament knows is the God of the resurrection." And just as our character apart from the grace of God cannot determine the Christian's hope, neither can outward circumstances decide the questions of the Christian's hope. "For I am sure," wrote the apostle Paul, "that neither death, nor life, nor angels, nor principalities, nor things present, nor things to come, nor powers, nor height, nor depth, nor anything else in all creation, will be able to separate us from the love of God in Christ Jesus our Lord" (Rom. 8:38–39, RSV).

This hope is reliable, also, because it is certified by the Holy Spirit within us. Samuel Johnson, the English author, was once asked by a woman, "How does one know when he has sinned?" Johnson replied, "A man knows when he has sinned, and that's that!" So it is with the presence of the Holy Spirit within us, creating hope. A man knows when the Holy Spirit is in his heart and life, and that's that! The Holy Spirit, of course does not make us infallible, does not guarantee that we shall never be discouraged, does not make us perfect beings. But even while we enjoy the knowledge that the Holy Spirit is in us, he is transforming us, making us into new and different and better persons. Assurance, confident assurance, and transformation of our lives go together. If a man claims to have the Holy Spirit within him and yet it makes no difference in how he thinks and lives and behaves toward other people, then his hope is false. "God's love has been poured into our hearts through the Holy Spirit which has been given to us." God loves us, and we love others. "We know that we have passed out of death into life, because we love the brethren" (1 John 3:14, RSV).

This hope can enable you and me to face life today undaunted. The ultimate enemy, death, cannot destroy our confident assurance that God will create "new heavens and a new earth." The crises that again and again burst rudely into our lives, such as failure in marriage, in business, or in health—these cannot destroy the bright confidence that God is doing great things in our lives even in the hour of our suffering. And certainly the little difficulties and vexations of everyday living are not too much for God, and what God has promised will make all of them more bearable, and actually shame us for our preoccupation with trivialities while God is offering his glory to us.

Accept the suffering of the present moment. Don't regard as the sign of God's rejection of you the pain that he lets you feel. Rather, look at it as a token of his acceptance. "For whom the Lord loveth he chasteneth, and scourgeth every son whom he receiveth" (Heb. 12:6). As theologian Karl Barth put it, "The gate at which all hope seems lost is the place at which it is continually renewed."

13
For the Mood of Skepticism

Habakkuk 1:1–24

"Yet I Will Rejoice"

Sometimes we don't know what to make of ourselves. We ought to be strong in faith, we feel, yet at times our faith is anything but strong. We become skeptical about how we stand with God, or about whether the Christian message is really true and does anything, or about God himself. Some persons would be quick to say this skepticism is un-American. Others would be almost as quick to say it is unchristian. But is faith something you can command, so that if you only try harder, if you practice believing several impossible things every morning before breakfast, you can even believe in God? The situation is very much like one I heard described. A patient in a hospital was shaking uncontrollably with a hysterical tremor while a well-meaning psychiatrist kept shouting at him, "Relax, John, relax!"

Should we condemn ourselves when the mood of skepticism settles in upon us? Should we feel guilty, as if we had committed some sort of unpardonable sin?

Before we are too hard on ourselves, before we place ourselves in the company of Voltaire, Paine, and Ingersoll, we ought to face one undeniable fact: the Bible itself is not only a book of faith, it is also a book of skepticism. The Bible is too honest to cover up the weaknesses and faults even of its best men and women. Though the heroes of the Bible scaled great heights of courage and daring and demonstrated amazing faith in God, these same heroes sometimes fell into chilling depths of doubt and hopelessness.

94

Listen to the plaint of the psalmist:

> Will the Lord spurn for ever,
>   and never again be favorable?
> Has his steadfast love for ever ceased?
>   Are his promises at an end for all time?
> Has God forgotten to be gracious?
>   Has he in anger shut up his compassion? (Ps. 77:7–9, RSV).

Listen to Job in his suffering lamenting:

> Oh, that I knew where I might find him,
>   that I might come even to his seat! (Job 23:3, RSV).

Listen to Habakkuk:

> O Lord, how long shall I cry for help,
>   and thou wilt not hear?
> Or cry to thee "Violence!"
>   and thou wilt not save? (Hab. 1:2, RSV).

Listen to John the Baptist, inquiring from prison of Jesus: "Are you he who is to come, or shall we look for another?" (Luke 7:20, RSV).

Listen to the disciple Thomas, saying of the risen Lord: "Unless I see in his hands the print of the nails, and place my finger in the mark of the nails, and place my hand in his side, I will not believe" (John 20:25, RSV).

Here are statements and questions that, except for the ancient setting and poetic style, might come from a recent discussion in a philosophy class on a university campus.

These are facts that we cannot hide in a closet. And we shouldn't want to. These facts are recorded for our encouragement.

If the Bible is a book of skepticism, it is also a book of faith. Faith is the more important thing. Doubt is but a shadow sometimes cast by faith. Yet true faith is often born in the throes of unbelief, despair, or doubt and refined and purified by them. Job said with throbbing confidence:

Behold, I go forward, but he is not there;
   and backward, but I cannot perceive him;
on the left hand I seek him, but I cannot behold him;
   I turn to the right hand, but I cannot see him.
But he knows the way that I take;
   when he has tried me, I shall come forth as gold (Job 23:8–10,
RSV).

Some have assumed that because the world has "come of age"
we can get along quite well without faith. Many are saying that
science can give us everything religion once promised, and more.
God belongs to our hierarchy of Western values as does Santa
Claus. But can we survive as a world, as a nation, as families,
or as individuals without faith? An old fable tells of a spider
that slid down a single filament of web from the high rafters
of a barn to a lower level where he established himself. He spread
his web, caught flies, prospered, and grew sleek and fat. One
Sunday afternoon as he wandered about, he looked at the single
filament that stretched up into the dark and said, "How useless!"
He snapped the thread, but his whole web came tumbling down
and was trampled underfoot. This kind of thing can happen to
us if we cut the cord of faith. Everything that makes life meaningful for us will collapse without faith in God and in his revelation
of himself.

This fact makes our skepticism a matter of urgent concern.
Doubt is only a step away from unbelief. What, then, can we
do about our doubts and skepticisms? Can we overcome them?

I

For one thing, we can wait hopefully for the answer to our
plight. This may be hard to do, for we are impatient. We want
an answer now! But sooner or later we have to agree with George
Meredith who said,

> Ah, what a dusty answer gets the soul
> When hot for certainties in this our life.

The trouble is, we may want God to answer in our own way, not his. We sometimes imagine that because the astronauts can go around the earth in the time it took our grandfathers to go across town and back, God ought to keep up-to-date and solve our difficulties with the speed of an electronic computer. But have we forgotten that some important things take just about as much time as they ever did? Recovery from a coronary thrombosis, the knitting of a broken bone, the birth of a child—all still take as long as they ever did.

Some of our modern, hammer-and-saw evangelism does not take this truth into account. A friend told me of a revival meeting he attended in a village church. At the close of the service a young man just back from military service was set upon by some tactless believers. He had made the mistake of telling them that he thought he was an atheist. They were determined to make a believer out of him whether God had anything to do with it or not. The air was blue with threats. If my friend had not rescued the young man, the poor fellow not only would have continued to think he was an atheist, he would have soon been sure of it and rejoiced. Don't forget that George Mueller prayed for two men for nearly sixty years, that they might become committed followers of Christ. One of them, we are told, was converted in the last service Mueller conducted and the other within six months after Mueller died.

Yet, should the fact that God takes his time in working out our doubts be any reason for a doubter to be blasé, or for any of us concerned about doubters to leave everything to God and do nothing ourselves? Pascal had it right when he said that there are only two kinds of people who are intelligent: those who serve God because they have found him, and those who are busy seeking him because they have not found him.

If you are plagued with doubts, wait patiently and hopefully for God to help you, but take care not to lose your concern.

II

In the second place, if we have doubts and skepticisms, we can trust the experience of others and be encouraged by their faith.

I thank God again and again for the men and women of faith I have known. I can't imagine where I would be today if it had not been for them. When I was weak, they were strong, and I leaned on their strength. When I had misgivings, they were confident, and I trusted their wisdom. They were, of course, as human as I was, with problems of their own, but they had character and faith and were like a tower of defense to me. I am not ashamed to acknowledge my debt to them.

At the same time, I am aware that I did not accept all of their beliefs simply because I accepted some of them, nor would they agree with all of mine. Even so, they helped me to believe what I believe, and I am grateful.

What was it that gripped Moses when God spoke to him at the back of the desert? Wasn't it God's identifying himself with Abraham, Isaac, and Jacob? The names of those men of faith awakened faith and awe in the heart of Moses. He saw himself as a part of that stream of history. Through them he was caught up into the purpose of God. He was full of doubts and fears, but one by one they fell away as the God of his fathers became more real to him, as he saw that this God about whom he had heard as a child was his God too. Many men and women believe today because of the faith of Martin Luther, John Wanamaker, Dorothy Sayers, Harry Emerson Fosdick, or T. S. Eliot.

There is a sense in which decision about God is a highly individual matter. This is what the existentialist philosophers and theologians keep telling us. There is no authentic being where there is no personal responsibility of decision. Yet we must not overlook that our decisions are never made in a vacuum. We are never completely alone when we make our agonizing decisions about God. It is as if unknown and unseen by us and surrounding us like the atmosphere are the friendly and encouraging voices and lives of thousands of others of all ages, speaking to our subconscious minds at a frequency where their presence and power are not obvious.

The letter to the Hebrews puts it well:

Therefore, since we are surrounded by so great a cloud of witnesses, let us also lay aside every weight, and sin which clings so closely, and let us run with perseverance the race that is set before us, looking to Jesus the pioneer and perfecter of our faith, who for the joy that was set before him endured the cross, despising the shame, and is seated at the right hand of the throne of God.

Consider him who endured from sinners such hostility against himself, so that you may not grow weary, or faint-hearted (12:1–3, RSV).

Who are these kind hearts that have been like guardian angels to us? We could begin with the first man or woman who worshiped God and passed that heritage down to us. We would have to include all those Hebrew prophets and people who saw God's hand in their life and celebrated his power and mercy with their witness. We would have to include Jesus Christ, the Word of God made flesh; the disciples who walked with him; and the plain people who welcomed his words of grace. We would have to include the apostolic fathers of the church, the Reformers, the evangelists, the pastors, and again the ordinary folk who believed what these persons said and proved it true in their own lives. We would have to include also our own fathers and mothers or those persons who brought God closest to us.

Remember, when you are overwhelmed with doubt, the total responsibility for discovering truth is not yours alone. You don't have to begin all over again and figure everything from scratch. Thousands upon thousands of friendly voices are trying to help us find the way, though our pride and our rebellion sometimes drown out their chorus of encouragement. These voices are all about us, and we are never alone.

III

Now in the third place, we can obey even when we cannot fully believe. As Dr. George Buttrick put it: "What we need is a strategy rather than a proof, a strategy and a certain valor of the spirit."

Wasn't this what Habakkuk had to come to? He wanted God to give him a satisfying answer to the evil he saw in the world, some justification of God in the face of man's inhumanity to man. Habakkuk was hot and angry about it all. He demanded that God give him an answer, and he climbed up on a watchtower in a vineyard and waited. The sun beat down on his brazen face and he waited. The wind whipped about the heap of stones where he stood and sat and knelt and stood again and waited. But the answer he had looked for until his eyes were red and strained and his spirit crushed did not come as he had hoped for it. But it came. It came, and how astonished he must have been at what it was!

It was no philosophy of good and evil that he got. It was a word that had the force of a command: "Behold, he whose soul is not upright in him shall fail, but the righteous shall live by his faith" (2:4, RSV).

We must not read the doctrine of justification by faith into these words prematurely, for this said to him: "Habakkuk, you ought to be concerned about one thing: your faithfulness to what you know to be right just now. God will take care of the problem of the wicked man in his own way. See to it that you are not one whose soul is not upright. You will live, you will survive the sifting of the good and the bad by your faithfulness, your loyalty to me even when you get no answer for your hectoring doubts. You may still be a skeptic, but you will have to be an obedient skeptic if you make it."

I read somewhere an old Latin saying, *solvitur ambulando* ("some things get solved just by going along with them"). Obey God today, and tomorrow you lose a fear; obey God tomorrow, and the next day you lose a doubt. You will remember that Jesus said, "If any man's will is to do his will, he shall know whether the teaching is from God or whether I am speaking on my own authority" (John 7:17, RSV).

Here is a mother who has haunting misgivings, but she is determined not to let her own misgivings keep her children from Christ. She obeys what God tells her is right in that situation, and she puts her little ones into the arms of Jesus Christ and finds her own faith strengthened as their faith grows and flowers. Or here is a businessman who finds his faith a matter of some amusement among his associates and sometimes wonders if they are right and he is wrong. He tries to bring what he feels to be the purpose of Christ into the tensions and ambiguities of the business world, and his faith grows in proportion to his commitment. Or here is a minister who takes Peter Boehler's advice to John Wesley: "Live *by* faith till you *have* faith." He doesn't surrender the possibility of certitude because he happens not to have it at the moment, but believes it is even for him, and at last he finds it.

Jesus Christ has baffled the minds of men and women through the ages. They have continued to ask, "What manner of man is this?" Some have fled from the mystery of his person and sought refuge in their doubts and fears. Others, just as skeptical at first, have said to him, "Lord, to whom shall we go? You have the words of eternal life." The same God confronts us in Christ today. As Albert Schweitzer put it: "He comes to us as One unknown, without a name, as of old, by the lakeside, He came to those

men who knew Him not . . . And to those who obey Him, . . .
he will reveal Himself in the toils, the conflicts, the sufferings
which they shall pass through in His fellowship, and as an ineffa-
ble mystery, they shall learn in their own experience Who He
is." [1]

[1] Albert Schweitzer, *The Quest of the Historical Jesus,* tr. by W. Montgomery (London:
Adam and Charles Black, 1948), p. 401.

14

What Can We Expect from God in a Crisis?

Daniel 3:17–18,26–27

"Our God . . . Is Able to Deliver Us"

Today, people in war-ravaged places could find comfort in the story of the three Hebrew children—if they knew it and believed it. The story belongs to such times and circumstances. Also, some of us may be facing personal crises in less violent circumstances, but matters of grave urgency nonetheless. How can *we* believe it and find there what will help *us?*

It is a strange story, assigned to the time when Nebuchadnezzar was king of Babylon in the sixth and seventh centuries B.C. It was written in its present form during a time of terrible persecution several centuries later. When we understand its spiritual lessons, its profound truth will amaze us. Like the book of Revelation, much is said between the lines which we might lose if we tried to understand it from a scientific or literal viewpoint. We will miss the point if we try to compare what happened with Wilmon Menard's gripping account of what he saw of the fire walkers on one of the islands of Tahiti. In the biblical story we have to do with God's way of dealing with his threatened people, not with some bizarre psychophysical phenomenon.

The story is simple. Three young Hebrews, men entrusted with certain government posts, refused to bow down and worship the golden image of a heathen god, even though the king ordered it. The king threatened to cast them into a burning fiery furnace. No matter! They trusted God to deliver them and so informed the king. However, they made it plain that if God did not choose to deliver them, they would still not bow to the king's order.

103

They were thrown into the furnace of fire, and while they were in it a fourth figure appeared—a divine figure. Then they came out intact, without even the smell of the flames upon them. As a result, King Nebuchadnezzar became a worshiper of their God.

What is God saying to us through this story? "I will be with you, my faithful people, when the fires of trouble get hotter and hotter for you." We can assume, therefore, that God will be with his faithful people in all their crises, whether they be great or small.

I

In our various life situations, God will compel us, as he did the young Hebrews, to confront the issues of decision. Choices have to be made. We may go along with no painful confrontations for a long, long time, but eventually we come up against matters that we cannot take for granted.

Sometimes the issue will be clear. It was so for the young men in our story. They were ordered to repudiate one of their most hallowed religious traditions, the conviction expressed in the ancient Shema: "Hear, O Israel: The Lord our God is one Lord." To bow in worship before the golden image would have signified their denial of the one Lord, Yahweh, creator of the heavens and the earth, the God of Israel. They had been cooperative at levels where their religious heritage and faith were not put in jeopardy, but they would not, they could not cooperate where they would have to deny their God. In the second century after Christ, Polycarp, a venerable Christian, faced such a choice when he was commanded by an authority to renounce Jesus Christ. He replied, "Eighty-six years have I served him, and he has never done me wrong. How can I now deny my King who has saved me?" Your life may not be threatened, but your job or your popularity may be at stake when someone with power over you demands that you violate what represents obedience to God in your life. The matter is clear-cut, and you may have to answer in the spirit of Martin Luther, "Here I stand . . . I can do no other . . . God help me! Amen."

But there are other times when the issue will be confused, when we are not confronted with a clear choice. We don't know, and perhaps cannot know at the time, what is the right course to follow. It is not a matter of our being double-minded persons, who are rightly regarded by James as unstable in all their ways. We are simply not infallible, and we do not at the time have the wisdom to make a decision that leaves no room for doubt. This is really where we often find ourselves. Well-meaning friends may be full of advice without really understanding all sides of our problem. We may, in addition, be in a temporary state of anxiety or depression which clouds the future with a pall of gloom and almost guarantees that our decision will be warped. Nevertheless, life has to go on, and we must decide on the basis of such knowledge as we have. We take seriously the best advice we can get and we try to leave our passing feelings as much as possible out of our decision. We know full well that we may be wrong, dreadfully wrong, but the time for decision has come; we would wait if we could, but we cannot.

II

However, we can trust God to help us make a good decision when matters of life and death, as well as matters of lesser importance, face us.

God gives courage to face the consequences of a right decision. Of course, we do not always know all of the consequences— good or bad—of a right decision. "If I had only known!" we sometimes lament in painful retrospect. But the three young Hebrews knew precisely what was in store for them. They knew that King Nebuchadnezzar made no idle threats. Yet they knew what the king did not know—that the true and living God had a stake in their faithfulness to him, that their God held the power of life and death not only over them, but also over Nebuchadnezzar, and that God could mightily use their example to strengthen others. I am sure that Helmut Thielicke knew that his criticism of Nazi policies could lead to his dismissal as professor at Heidelberg. It happened, and when he protested his dismissal the Nazi officer told him, "As long as there are any faculties of theology left—and it won't be much longer, sir—I shall see to it that only sucking pigs and no wild boars are given professorships." Yet Thielicke survived without his professorship, having faced the consequences of his decision with such courage as God gave him.

But what happens when we have to make a decision in some gray area, when right and wrong do not stand out in such stark contrast as black and white? This is where many of us have to live every day. Some of us do not enjoy the luxury of a simplistic ethic. Theologian Reinhold Niebuhr said:

The love of God and the love of self are curiously intermingled in life. The worship of God and the worship of self confronts us in a multitude of different compounds. There is a taint of sin in our highest endeavors. How shall we judge the great statesman who gives a nation its victorious courage by articulating its only partly conscious and implicit resources of fortitude; and who mixes the most obvious forms of personal and collective pride and arrogance with this heroic fortitude? If he had been a more timid man, a more cautious soul, he would not have sinned so greatly, but neither would he have wrought so nobly.[1]

In these days, none of us can hope to live with a comfortable conscience. Life is too complex and we are too involved in everything about us to have a comfortable conscience. But we can have a comforted conscience, knowing that the grace of God will cover our imperfections. We have to learn that absolute faithfulness is not in the final analysis what moves God to help us. We can trust God to give us courage to make some kind of responsible decision.

III

Where can we find the necessary bravery to carry through when we must decide? It is simply in the assurance that God will be with us whatever may come.

Though the main question is not deliverance, he often does deliver us. "Deliver us from evil" is a legitimate prayer. James asserted, "The prayer of faith shall save the sick." The four Gospels are full of stories of God's deliverance of individuals from physical ills. All of us have known of persons who credited their recovery from sickness or their escape from danger to God's intervention. Shadrach, Meshach, and Abednego believed that God could deliver them from the wrath of King Nebuchadnezzar, and God used them to show that he was superior to all earthly powers. Perhaps their faith was shaken a bit when they were bound hand and foot and brought to the furnace of fire and yet no sign of God's deliverance appeared. But God did deliver them—in a way they did not expect. God can and does often literally answer our prayers. With God all things are possible.

But we must not think that God has to deliver us literally from all evil, all suggestion of harm. We can hardly insist that the writer of the book of Daniel would have us believe that. The second book of Maccabees, describing events that occurred during the very time the book of Daniel was written, tells the story of seven brothers who died in flames one after the other for their faith in God and their loyalty to him. Their mother said to the seventh of them, as he made ready to die: "Accept death, so that in God's mercy I may get you back again with your brothers." So he died, as did the others, believing that "the King of the universe will raise us up to an everlasting renewal of life, because we have died for his laws."

The main question is this: the presence of God with us regardless. The young Hebrews could not be sure that God would spare

them from the flames of the king's wrath; they could only be
sure that God would be with them in the midst of the flames
or anywhere else. The proud, gloating king, looking into the fiery
furnace saw not three figures, but four, and the fourth looked
like a divine figure—"a god," Nebuchadnezzar called him. How
true to the words of the psalmist!

> Whither shall I go from thy Spirit?
>   Or whither shall I flee from thy presence?
> If I ascend to heaven, thou art there?
>   If I make my bed in Sheol, thou art there!
> If I take the wings of the morning
>   and dwell in the uttermost parts of the sea,
> even there thy hand shall lead me,
>   and thy right hand shall hold me (139:7–10, RSV).

And how comfortingly true when one turns not away from God
but toward him in obedience or in some daring venture of faith!
God does not have to spare us from suffering, pain, rejection,
and persecution—if only he be with us in it! God may deny us
some things, even life, that he may give us himself and all that
the gift of himself includes.

[1] Reinhold Niebuhr, *Discerning the Signs of the Times* (New York: Charles Scribner's
Sons, 1946), pp. 191–92.

15

The Gift of Courage

Joshua 1:1–9

"God Is with You"

The audience in the packed lecture hall, educators from many countries, stood and responded with wave after wave of applause after a moving address by Dr. Viktor Frankl. It was 1965, and the University of Vienna was celebrating its 600th anniversary. Dr. Frankl, a member of the medical faculty, had spoken on his favorite theme, which was the passion and explanation of his life, "the will to meaning."

I was there, and I believe I know why the audience responded that day with such fervor. It was not only because of what the speaker said, though it was meaty and well-prepared. Nor was it just because of the exciting delivery, though a friend turned to me and said with a twinkle, "He spoke like a Texas evangelist, didn't he?" The real reason, I feel, was profound admiration of the courage that had brought this Jewish psychiatrist through unspeakable suffering. He had endured the death of his father, mother, brother, and wife at the hands of the Nazis. As a prisoner he had known the horrors of the death camp himself, but he had survived with a bit of luck and the courage that a conviction of meaning in life had given him.

Most of us do not find ourselves in circumstances that call for the raw, incredible courage demanded of men and women who have had everything good and worthwhile taken away from them. Life treats us far more kindly. But we all, young and old alike, have experiences that call for courage just as real as the spirit demanded of the martyrs. And to us, as well as to Joshua, come words that can transform our cowardice into courage. Some of us have heard these words many times and up till now have taken them only half-seriously. They sound good and inspirational, and that's the end of it! But hear them again! This time they might lead to some important change in your life—who knows? "Be strong and of a good courage" (KJV); "Be strong, be resolute" (NEB).

Can you imagine how desperately Joshua needed such a command? Moses was dead, and the leadership of a migrant nation had fallen on Joshua's shoulders. Before him lay the Promised Land with its treasures and its dangers. Who was a match for this challenge? Not Joshua! He was only human, and he knew his weaknesses better than anyone else. But God was God, and he said, "Be strong and of a good courage." This made the great difference. If you take it seriously, it can make a profound difference in your life.

Where can we, we who also know our weakness, get what it takes to act bravely in face of temptation and trial? To endure suffering and persecution, to take up a new job, to live through a divorce, to survive private guilt or public disgrace, and, just as importantly, to have a first date, to get one's first job, to marry and build a home, to bring children into the world, to retire, to lose loved ones and friends, and ultimately to face one's own death? Who holds the magic key to courage needed to see us through?

I

To begin with, the secret lies within ourselves.

Courage is a native gift. We are born with it, and it stays with us as long as we live, even though we don't call on it often enough.

What is courage? It is that quality of character that will help us to stand firm or push on even when life goes against us. It is what will help us to endure anxiety or pain to reach our goals.

Courage is not simply a spiritual quality. It is physical as well. Fear is an inborn instinct, but so is courage. Religious people and nonreligious people alike know what it means to be afraid; and both groups again and again show surprising resources of courage. The instinct for self-preservation has been widely recognized. Our adrenal glands react to danger and tend to make us do one of two things—fight or run. They can support our courage, our caution, or our cowardice.

Courage, such as it is, serves on many levels of life. You may find yourself at this very moment in a situation where raw courage, no more than is within reach, is called for. Robert Louis Stevenson said, "You cannot run away from a weakness; you must some time fight it out or perish; and if that be so, why not now, and where you stand?"

An Australian physician, Mrs. Claire Weekes, has declared that one can refuse to run away, can fight it out, and can win a victory, despite weakness, trembling, panic, and despair. The resources within your physical body come into play, trembling has an end, panic subsides—only stand firm! It has been pointed out that some imperiled marriages last because of the sheer determination to make them last. One could go on to say that bravery in battle, willingness to deny self, serving one's fellowmen against almost intolerable opposition—all these acts of courage can come from resources that we are born with, resources that we have quietly cultivated bit by bit through the years. Admiral Drake, we are told, stood on his quarterdeck before a battle, shaking all over, and remarked: "My flesh trembles at the many dangers into which my resolute heart will lead me." So you and I may stand and, while trembling, be "strong and of a good courage." In the words of William James, "He who, with Marcus Aurelius, can truly say, 'O Universe, I wish all that thou wishest,' has a self from which every trace of negativeness and obstructiveness has been removed—no wind can blow except to fill its sails." And some one might even say, with no irreverence intended:

> I am the master of my fate;
> I am the captain of my soul.

II

So courage comes from within ourselves. But not only so. Courage comes from others.

If we are courageous at all, it is because others have helped us to be steadfast and resolute.

The apostle Paul, as we all know, had no easy time of it. Life was hard on him. But many people along the way made it easier: he could take heart and keep going. One man, Onesiphorus, is singled out for special praise. "He cheered me up many times," Paul said. "He was not ashamed that I am in prison, but as soon as he arrived in Rome he started looking for me until he found me" (2 Tim. 1:16–17, TEV). As a teenager, I heard a story I could not forget. A destructive fire was roaring. The firemen had fought hard to evacuate the burning building. Only one person, waiting frantically at a window several stories from the ground, remained to be rescued. A fireman on a long laqder struggled to get the person to safety and was about to fail. A man standing below turned to the crowd of spectators and cried, "Give him a cheer!" Up went a tumultuous cheer. The fireman on the ladder found new strength and brought the person to safety. Who knows what miracles have been wrought by a fitting word, by a firm handclasp, or by some simple act of brotherly kindness?

Courage comes from others also in a slightly different way. It comes when we discover our common bond of humanity; when we discover that in many ways we are all in the same boat. But this is not too easy to see. We walk about comparing ourselves unfavorably with other people, comparing our worst with their best. We feel unworthy, inferior, and weak, and this makes us cowardly. It makes it hard for us to improve ourselves. Churches can do this to people. That is what caused Henry Ward Beecher, one of the best known churchmen of the nineteenth century, to say emphatically that the church is not a gallery for displaying eminent Christians, but a school for training imperfect ones. One of the secrets of the phenomenal success of Alcoholics Anonymous lies in its ability to help men and women to discover our common bond of humanity, to recognize that people who have special problems can strengthen one another, and to believe that there is a God who wants to save us from our private misery. When we are in church and the minister is talking about either guilt or goodness, we can make the mistake of saying, "He is talking about me," or "He is talking about him." It is often more helpful to say, "He is talking about us."

The letter to the Hebrews says that we should "be concerned for one another, to help one another to show love and to do good" (Heb. 10:25, TEV). Many times this is just how some struggling man or woman finds the courage to keep going.

Professor William Lyon Phelps, a beloved and world renowned teacher at Yale, during his lifetime endured at least two periods of protracted black despair. As a result, he was always sympathetic with sufferers from "nerves" or from melancholia or depression, for, as he said, "I know the particular part of hell they are in." He felt when any young person committed suicide that if someone could only have been with him, this young person might have had before him forty or fifty years of happiness. Many times our own courage is not sufficient. If we are of good courage, if we are resolute, if we stand fast, it must be together with one or more persons who lend us their strength, or even, so to speak, their weakness, which may become strength to us.

III

We have to go one step further. Courage comes from God. In the last analysis, of course, in every case! But it can happen also in the immediate situation.

When some sea too deep confronts us as it did the Israelites and Moses, God has the decisive word. When a future threatening with uncertainty and danger confronts us as it did the Israelites and Joshua, God again has the decisive word. Personal opinion and personal courage, the consensus of our friends and their frenzy to fight do not settle things when matters of life and death are decided. We rely then on the promise of God. Sometimes the promise of God is all we have to go on. We feel no strength inside us. No one helpful appears in the hour of crisis. Only God and his word are there. But most often God's promise mobilizes our own courage and solidifies the help of our comrades in arms. We hear the words, "Be strong and of a good courage," and all is well.

Still, we have more than a naked promise to rely on. Experience of God's mercies shows that every promise is true. Things may be tough for you now, but has he ever failed you or forsaken you? I did not ask, Did God ever let you feel disappointed or suffer? I asked, Did God ever really cast you aside with no consolations, with nothing worth hoping for? Time has unraveled many a problem, time has brought many compensations, time has prepared you for new and perhaps even more trying experiences. The apostle Paul wrote to the Corinthians of misfortune that befell him in Asia. He said, "We were so utterly, unbearably crushed that we despaired of life itself. Why, we felt that we had received the sentence of death; but that was to make us rely not on ourselves but on God who raises the dead; he delivered us from so deadly a peril, and he will deliver us; on him we have set our hope that he will deliver us again" (2 Cor. 1:8–10, RSV).

We too can stand fast singly or together, expecting God to be with us. We can be strong and of a good courage, for God will help us. God will be with us and help us to face both moral and physical danger. And there is plenty of each!

All of us have to live amid moral uncertainties. Right and wrong are not always clear. Just to live in this world is to be involved in sin. Our choices are often not between right and wrong, but between two degrees of wrong or right, and as responsible persons we have to choose. How can we do it? Martin Luther once wrote to a friend and colleague: "Sin boldly!" Strange advice! But he did not mean, as it would be easy to suppose, that anyone should deliberately choose an evil way. He meant that even though there is some mixture of evil in the best things we can do, we should live courageously and joyfully, depending on God's grace to see us through. "Believe even more boldly," he said, "in the forgiveness of Christ."

God will not let any of us, if we truly belong to him, live with a comfortable conscience. Too much of the world, life, and human relationships is riddled with evil. But he will give us a comforted conscience, so that we can move bravely ahead, trying the best we can to serve him, though we make a thousand mistakes doing it. We can say with the psalmist, "Yea, though I walk through the valley of the shadow of death, I will fear no evil; for thou art with me; thy rod and thy staff, they comfort me." And we can pray with John Henry Newman as well:

> Keep Thou my feet; I do not ask to see
> The distant scene, one step enough for me.

Now suppose we recognize the many different gifts of courage that are already ours or that are freely offered and available to us. Does this mean that sweeping, dramatic changes will take place in our lives? No, not necessarily. But it does mean that we will at least live our lives on a deeper level; that we will not be so often defeated; that when we are defeated we will get back to our feet much sooner; and that instead of always thinking about our own problems, we will be more concerned to help others with theirs.

In Bunyan's *Pilgrim's Progress,* we find a striking picture of our human situation. As we make our pilgrimage, we come to a narrow passageway, and lions are lying in the way (they are chained, but we do not see their chains). Like the characters, Timorous and Mistrust, we are tempted, panic-stricken, to turn back, but we hear the voice that says, "Keep in the midst of the path, and no hurt shall come unto thee." And we find it to be true. When we are commanded, "Be strong and of a good courage," it is not empty advice; it is not a challenge to lift ourselves by our heels. It is the word of the Lord, and with the command comes the power to obey. "Turn not . . . to the right hand or to the left, that you may have good success wherever you go. Have I not commanded you? Be strong and of good courage; be not frightened, neither be dismayed; for the Lord your God is with you wherever you go" (Josh. 1:7,9, RSV).

16
Foolish Fatalism

Revelation 19:6

"The Lord . . . Reigns"

Let me begin this sermon with some blunt questions. Is what you are doing right now with your life determined by a defeatist attitude that you have taken toward some moral mistake you have made in the past? Or a physical handicap? Or a failure in your business or professional career? Or the kind of home or community you grew up in?

Do you ever feel as Edna St. Vincent Millay when she compared her life to the gnawing of a mouse, writing of the endless boredom of living day after day in the same old place? Or as Ecclesiastes pessimistically puts it?

> The sun rises and the sun goes down,
>> and hastens to the place where it rises.
>
> . . . .
>
> What has been is what will be,
>> and what has been done is what will be done;
>> and there is nothing new under the sun (Eccl. 1:5,9, RSV).

The truth is, fatalism can take hold of us, like a cold, clammy hand out of the night. The ground is already laid for our cringing and cowering in terror before life. Just being born into this big world peopled with giants is enough to make one afraid. It is not hard for a child, we are told, to believe wild stories of giants, for this is the world he knows. More than half the people he knows tower above him. But time goes on. The thought of worlds upon worlds and limitless space dawns upon us. Then we may suffer from what has been called "cosmic intimidation." One man cried out what many other men have thought when he said, "When I consider thy heavens, the work of thy fingers, the moon and stars, which thou hast ordained; What is man that thou art mindful of him? and the son of man, that thou visitest him" (Ps. 8:3).

However, what bothers us most, what makes us terribly weak, is not what the world or the universe or nature or whatever does to us. What bothers us most is what happens to some of us, while others go scot-free; what we do to ourselves that others are not so foolish as to do to themselves. We are troubled because we had two strikes against us to start with, because we took the one chance we had and played a kind of moral Russian roulette with it and lost, or because some misfortune came bearing down on us out of nowhere and put us out of commission. What has that done to us then? Some of us are plodding, like blind Samson, in an imprisoning treadmill of a job we hate with a passion. Some of us are tampering with alcohol or drugs as a temporary escape from guilt and discouragement. Some of us are wearing ourselves out with unnecessary illnesses that mask the humiliation of our defeat. And the more we think about it, the worse off we are.

We are reminded of the mother in a store's toy department. Examining a toy, she noted that it was complicated for a child. The clerk explained, "It's an educational toy designed to equip a child to live in the modern world—no matter how he puts it together it won't work!" Yet we know that some persons have not capitulated to their misfortunes, whether these misfortunes were of their own making or were nobody's fault. We know that Julius Caesar had epilepsy, that Charles Darwin was an invalid, that Lord Nelson had only one eye, that Beethoven became deaf, that John Milton became blind, that Charles Steinmetz was a hunch-back, that Robert Louis Stevenson had tuberculosis.[1] We know, also, that the apostle Paul once made havoc of the church and that Anton Boisen, a pioneer in training the clergy to minister to sick souls, was once insane himself. We know this, and it both troubles us and gives us a hint of encouragement. Those persons were individuals who, if they had looked at life as some of us look at it, would never have made their mark.

As you look at the lives of the great achievers, you discover that the secret of their success morally and spiritually, as well as otherwise, was that they refused to take No for an answer as they stood up to life. They could hear the imperious *yes* of God thundering through all the petty noises and irritations of their lives. A frozen fate melted before the warmth of the proffered grace of God.

Some took the route of direct attack on their problems. And there are certain situations that yield to the method of direct attack. A streptococcus infection yields to attack by penicillin, and when the patient recovers, he may be as sound as ever. A financial failure may teach a businessman valuable lessons, and he may be more successful than ever because he suffered a temporary setback. And most astounding of all, an individual has been sometimes better and more useful to God and to mankind because pride was broken in a humiliating moral lapse and that man or woman learned that only God is God. In each of these cases, the person saw a specific problem, struggled with it, and solved it. And now that person is happy in victory.

On the other hand, some people must face the fact that direct attack will do no good. With grief, the amputee must surrender to the brutal truth that all his efforts will not restore the limb he lost. The bereaved mother cannot bring back her beloved child. The prodigal cannot relive his wasted years. To realize such a fact, to know in one's heart that this is actually true, is oftentimes enough to paralyze the will, to tempt one to take the advice of Job's wife to "curse God and die" (Job 2:9).

However, most people do not quite give up. They may yearn

with Louisa Fletcher Tarkington for "the Land of Beginning Again, a place where mistakes, heartaches, and selfish grief "can be dropped like a shabby old coat . . . and never put on again."

And thank God, there is such a land. Any man, any woman, any young person who feels the pain of the past or the paralysis of the present can have things different. Matters do not have to be as they are. Some things about your situation may never change, but the important issue is, Will *you* change? Will you let yourself be changed?

If any person ever had reason to quit, to surrender to his failure, to live with his head bowed down as he went slinking along the streets, it was Saul of Tarsus. He had persecuted the church, God's own people. And there were many bitter people ready to remind him of it, even years later. The cloud of this guilt could easily have shut out forever the light of the sun, moon, and stars of God's love. But he refused to let it happen. He refused to let it cripple his efforts to get others to know that love. And all over the Roman Empire men and women were in his debt for their faith in Jesus Christ. But he explained his attitude quite simply when he declared: "By the grace of God I am what I am, and his grace toward me was not in vain" (1 Cor. 15:10, RSV).

Here is the redeeming truth: The creator God, the redeeming God, the God who makes all things new is trying to break through our stubborn fatalism—whether it is pleasure in self-punishment or paralysis of the will in defeat—trying to break through and throw open the gates of new life to us.

Listen to what God said to defeated Israel during the days of the Exile, for he may be saying it to you: "And I will multiply upon you man and beast; and they shall increase and be fruitful; and I will cause you to be inhabited as in your former times, and will do more good to you than ever before. Then you will know that I am the Lord" (Ezek. 36:11, RSV).

Well, what can you and I do about it? The business of waiting for God to do everything can be another kind of paralyzing fatalism.

I

One thing we can do is to decide, to commit ourselves. A friend of mine, a psychologist, has said that the problems of those he counseled centered more in indecision than in anything else. And that is understandable. The momentous decisions of life are not made with the flip of a coin.

On December 29, 1869, William James, later a professor at Harvard University, wrote a letter to his novelist brother, Henry: "I have been a prey to such disgust of life during the past three months as to make letter writing almost an impossibility . . . My own condition, I am sorry to say, goes on pretty steadily deteriorating in all respects . . ."

William James's great problem was a kind of fatalism, in which he was almost completely convinced that he was doomed to live a useless, drifting, ineffectual life because of his very elusive physical and emotional illness. But almost four months later to the day, he recorded in his diary: "I think that yesterday was a crisis in my life. I finished the first part of Renouvier's second *Essais* and see no reason why his definition of free will—'the sustaining of a thought *because I choose to* when I might have other thoughts'— need be the definition of an illusion. At any rate, I will assume for the present—until next year—that it is no illusion. My first act of free will shall be to believe in free will." This was a real turning point in James's life, the beginning point for a steady, though long-drawn-out, struggle and victory over the shattering results of a foolish fatalism. When he saw that he had a decisive role in his future and that he was free to play it, then everything became different.

If there is anything the New Testament makes plain, it is that every man, every woman must break out of the vicious, self-defeating circle by a personal decision; "for God is at work in you, both to will and to work for his good pleasure" (Phil. 2:13, RSV). The apostle Paul could never have said, "By the grace of God I am what I am," if he had not personally decided one day to let that divine favor have its way in his life from that time forth.

Studdert-Kennedy, the colorful chaplain of World War I, said that Christ keeps on challenging us until at last we can build the "Is" with the brick of the "Might 'ave been."

II

Not only must we decide, we must also forget the failures, the humiliations, the embarrassments. This is the dimension of decision that has to do with the past. It is a foolish fatalism to permit the days and experiences that are gone to blackmail us for the rest of our lives. And we do not have to. "If any one is in Christ, he is a new creation; the old has passed away, behold, the new has come" (2 Cor. 5:17, RSV). The mercy and forgiveness of God removes our guilt like a vast incinerator that consumes the germ-breeding garbage of a city.

III

Not only must we decide and forget, but we must also listen to the inner voice daily, lest the old cynical, defeatist, fatalistic voices snare our attention again. Listening to the inner voice is the dimension of decision that has to do with the future. It is a foolish fatalism to imagine that Jesus Christ has nothing new and fresh to say to us every day we live. We must listen to hear what he has to say about the big decisions that come once or twice in a lifetime, and we must listen to hear what he has to say about the vexing little problems of everyday living. Unless the claim of the future is stronger than the claim of the past, we may little by little slip back into our dark cavern of fatalism.

Consider how this worked out in the life of one man. His past was loaded with gruesome memories. The future was threatening. He hardly knew what to do and covered up his indecision with increasing anger and aggressiveness. He was at the breaking point. Then something happened. The living Christ came over his life, like the Spirit of God that brooded upon the chaos at the dawn of creation. A new man was born. Now there was comfort and hope and certitude. Saul of Tarsus was gone forever. Paul, a man in Christ, was there to plow his way into history unforgettably.

Is there one now saying, "God knows my life needs to be different? I want to know the presence of Jesus Christ in my life and hear his voice. How do I get to know God or get to know him better?"

The answer is simple: Go where Jesus Christ is, and then you will know his presence, and there you can hear his voice.

But where is he? Well, we trust that he is among his people. Many a person has come to know the presence of Christ and hear his voice by worshiping among his people. But some do not. If you do not, then I remind you that our Lord said that he was to be found among the hungry, the thirsty, the strangers, the ill-clad, and the prisoners.

Perhaps the reason that your religion has gone stale is that you have kept looking for him in a house of worship when, so far as you are concerned, he has moved on to another place where he wants you to be with him. And it may be that some of us will never really find him again in the house of worship until we find him abiding, as he said we could, among the most despised, exploited, and unfortunate people on earth.

I believe in the church—the church universal and the church local. I believe in it despite its chronic weaknesses and its obvious failures. I have no desire to throw stones at it simply because that is a popular pastime of some persons. But I am convinced that some of us will never really know the Christ of the New Testament until we follow him from the safety of the sanctuary into the dangers of daily discipleship, where faith is costly and external rewards are few or nonexistent. We *will* know him, however, if we follow him, go where he goes, and do what he wills.

If you imagine that life cannot be different for you, then you have not reckoned on God, for with his invincible grace God can overcome the worst that life can do to us, "for the Lord God omnipotent reigneth" (Rev. 19:6).

[1] Charles L. Allen, *In Quest of God's Power* (Westwood, N.J.: Fleming H. Revell Co., 1952), p. 28.

17

Mercy—Withheld or Given?

Matthew 5:7

"Blessed Are the Merciful"

A church leader walked through an airport terminal. A man
with an outstretched hand approached him for help. The man
staggered as if drunk, and the church leader hurried on, too busy
to waste time on a drunk. Later, to his dismay, he learned that
the man had had a heart attack and was reaching out for help.
Mercy withheld!

A writer who had researched the corporate scene described
how some persons become successful executives. One thing essential, he said, is that the rising executive be able—ruthlessly, if
necessary—to discard any associates or subordinates that stand
in his way of getting ahead; he must be able to do this without
losing a wink of sleep. Mercy withheld!

This kind of thing doesn't go on only in the so-called "secular
world." It affects both minister and layman within the church.
We in the church have taken our lessons from this world and
have often learned them only too well. The church has caught
the spirit of a success-crazy generation whose values are linked
to increased production, higher wages, and greater consumption
of goods. Success is determined by increases that can be measured
in dollars and cents. We apply the same yardstick to the church.
Now, Christianity with its many institutions *is* big business—
let's not forget that! And modern efficiency can help the church
in many ways. But sometimes callousness and ruthlessness come
with efficiency. The organization—the machine—becomes more
important than persons. The minister is crucified because he does

not seem to succeed; the layman is crucified because he is just a statistic or because he does not seem to fit into the machine. An ever-bigger and more efficient ecclesiastical Juggernaut may roll on, while there seems to be less and less need for God and prayer and compassion and ethics. The individual counts for nothing. Mercy withheld!

So, inside the walls of the church and outside, we have opportunities to help or to hurt, to show mercy or to withhold it.

A fitting word for such a state of affairs is Jesus' beatitude: "Blessed are the merciful, for they shall obtain mercy." We may be tempted to apply these words to a future manifestation of the kingdom. If we do so, we should ask if we are not trying to bring our interpretation and doctrine in line with our personal weaknesses. However, it is more likely that we will rid ourselves of the demands of this verse by simply ignoring it. Still, if we can be honest with ourselves now, will you face with me what it means to show mercy? Can we become truly merciful persons? Let us see.

I

To get at this problem, let us consider, to begin with, this question: Who is in a position to be merciful? We can say right off that it is usually persons who for one reason or another are for the moment in a superior position. They have the upper hand. They can help someone who needs help, someone who perhaps has forfeited every claim to help, someone whom they could hurt not only through neglect but also by deliberate design.

We can see this in a familiar story told by our Lord. Jesus' parable of the good Samaritan hints of two kinds of cruelty: the cruelty of the robbers who beat a poor man and left him to die and the cruelty of the religious leaders who left the dying man unattended alongside the road while they hurried on to their prayers and their songs. The parable tells us also of mercy extended. Another man came along. He—a foreigner—stopped to help. Race or nationality, bodily or financial risk—these things meant nothing, for a man needed help, and there was no one else to give it.

II

But how well are we getting along at showing mercy? We are merciful; we couldn't stand the sight of our face in the mirror if we were completely without mercy. We imagine that we would never pass up a case of genuine need or be intentionally unmerciful. But is this really so?

We can say this for ourselves: we are merciful if it is convenient. We can be very merciful if it doesn't interrupt our schedule, if it doesn't cost too much, and especially if enough people might discover our charity. So we may continue year after year giving money to beggars, but may never give fifteen minutes to ferret out their deepest need. And we may eagerly snatch sinners as "brands from the burning" only to leave them close enough to the fire to fall in again.

We are merciful, also, if we can keep our mercy within the bounds of reason. We know that true mercy is not mere sentimentality; it has backbone; it is ethical. We know that unbridled generosity of any kind can be demoralizing, that it can defeat its purpose. So we temper our mercy with justice, and thus we sometimes disguise our hardness of heart. Lazarus lies at our door. But we must not do too much for him; it might spoil him; he might not be ready for health and dignity; the community is used to seeing him in his filth and to recoiling from his odor, and it is not prepared to accept him. Let's not do him an injustice by helping him too much! And so we are merciful up to a point.

Again, we are merciful if somehow the recipient is tuned to our own religious, social, or political viewpoint. If someone stands athwart the highway of God, arms akimbo, defying the onward march of his servants, then we are ready to call down fire from heaven to clear a path for our God. It may not really matter what this person is or who he is: he qualifies as God's opponent if he disagrees with us. Or we may be more fair than that: possibly we have no personal axe to grind; we may have God's cause genuinely at heart. But we may take up arms against the supposed enemy of God with weapons God has long since disowned.

So we are merciful—after a fashion.

III

But does this modified mercy reflect God's will for us? We can best answer this question by taking a good, long look at the mercy of God himself. What is his mercy like?

God's mercy? Where our mercy operates now and then, the mercy of God never fails. The psalmist sang of the faithfulness of God's mercy toward his people: "for his mercy endureth forever." God made a covenant with his people—his chosen people— and he kept it in all the changing conditions of their lives. He kept it when they forgot it; when by their lives they denied it. The steadfast love of God ruled and overruled their lives by day and by night, in the wilderness and in the land of promise, in the exile and in the return. The children of Israel belonged to God in a special way, and he stuck by them. The Old Testament shows that God showered such love uniquely upon Israel; he had not so bound himself to any other people. Where God had obligated himself by love, by purpose, and by promise, his faithfulness never wavered. No inconvenience, no embarrassment, no risk kept him from doing what he had set out to do. "He that keepeth thee will not slumber. Behold he that keepeth Israel shall neither slumber nor sleep" (Ps. 121:3–4). Isn't this the kind of mercy that we ought to show toward those that duty and love tell us to help? But this is not all.

Where we often dole out our mercy grudgingly, the mercy of God is extravagant. Paul shows us, in the epistle to the Romans, how God can be both merciful and just; how there is no wrong in God's forgiveness: God's mercy is thoroughly ethical. This stands out in the New Testament: the overwhelming extravagance of God's mercy. What a risk God took in offering his mercy apart from "works of righteousness which we have done" (Titus 3:5)! "Where sin abounded, grace did much more abound" (Rom. 5:20). Even so, we sometimes become the gloomy heralds of Good News; the stingy dispensers of the grace of God, when we ought to be saying to the most unpromising of men and women, "The mercy of God is for you—especially for you." But we can say more.

Where our mercy is reserved for our friends, the mercy of God goes out even to his enemies. "He maketh his sun to rise on the evil and on the good, and sendeth rain on the just and on the unjust" (Matt. 5:45). Recall the words of Portia in Shakespeare's *The Merchant of Venice:*

> The quality of mercy is not strain'd,
> It droppeth as the gentle rain from heaven
> Upon the place beneath. It is twice bless'd:
> It blesseth him that gives and him that takes.
>
> It is an attribute to God himself;
> And earthly power doth then show likest God's,
> When mercy seasons justice.

Jesus held up the perfection of God's mercy as the model for his followers: "Love your enemies, bless them that curse you, do good to them that hate you, and pray for them which despitefully use you and persecute you" (Matt. 5:44). Surely we must confess, as we look at the quality and quantity of our mercy, that it is far, far short of the excellence of God's mercy. It is a pretty discouraging comparison, isn't it?

IV

So, what are our chances of becoming people who can be counted on to show mercy when mercy is called for?

If there is a way, we must find it. And why? Because God's mercy is most often known through the merciful acts of human beings; because God's kingdom tarries at the barrier of our hardness of heart; and because our own salvation, our own spiritual maturity is tied up with this business of mercy. In giving we receive; in forgetting self, we find life eternal. "Blessed are the merciful, for *they* shall obtain mercy."

There is a way, but not an easy way. Being merciful without exception, without measure, without limits—this comes hard to us; it is not natural to us; we would not seek it on our own. Being merciful *is* possible to us if we have already received mercy or if we will receive it. Our text—the fifth Beatitude—follows four others that John Wick Bowman believed to make four clear, basic steps to God. Dr. Bowman said that the keynotes of these Beatitudes are to be found in these words: realization, repentance, trust, and salvation.

At any rate, if I am a truly merciful person, it is not necessarily because I was born tenderhearted; it is more likely because I have received mercy, because someone showed me how to be merciful by being merciful to me. To show mercy is worship, for worship is my response to God's mercy toward me. It is better than a hymn or a prayer or a sermon. It is a gift in kind to the glory of God. I cannot really give God anything through a burnt offering, through some arbitrary self-sacrifice, or through loud protestations of gratitude. But I can give to God if, through gratitude for mercy received, I am merciful to someone else. A layman who gave generous help to a college student explained to me why he did it: "A man who helped me to go to college told me that he didn't want me to pay him back. He said that he would be repaid if someday I helped some other student go to college."

We can see this truth clearly in the epistle to the Ephesians: "Let all bitterness, and wrath, and anger, and clamour, and evil speaking, be put away from you, with all malice: And be ye kind one to another, tenderhearted, forgiving one another, even as God for Christ's sake hath forgiven you" (4:31–32). A life of mercy is the flowering of gratitude for mercy received.

If you and I succeed in showing forth the mercy of God, we must often ponder its meaning in our own lives. We can be helped by coming to the communion table always with deliberation, with self-examination, with confession, and with renewal of commitment. We can be helped, too, by daily reflecting upon the wonder of God's mercy.

How long has it been since you actually confessed your sins to God and gratefully acknowledged your utter dependence on his mercy? Have we reduced the gospel to a system to be grasped intellectually only? Have we so mastered the Bible that we have denied its judgment of us? Have we ceased to be gripped by the gospel's sweeping marvel—the mercy that melts the heart, that gives life a new point of beginning, that moves out into the world in ever-widening circles, encompassing the deepest needs of humanity? If so, then we must go and stand again on the holy ground before the cross, and stand there until the flaming light of Jesus' sacrifice kindles within us a fire to warm the hearts of all kinds of people everywhere—by making us merciful!